Relationships REDEFINED

Learn the Art of Prioritizing Relationships

Akanksha Rastogi

INDIA • SINGAPORE • MALAYSIA

ISBN 979-8-88546-876-3

Dedication

Ever since I was young, I have enjoyed composing poetry and writing short stories. As a young adult and to this day, I have been consistently blogging, which has helped me gain widespread recognition beyond the confines of my own country among the variety of readers across the multitude of cultures throughout the globe. This book is an attempt to take my passion and dreams to the next level and spread my "World of Words" into people's bookshelves and into 'their' worlds.

The origin of this book is owed to a blend of thoughts derived from my life's learnings and my parents' blessings. I am a proud daughter to a Journalist mother, Smt. Abha Rastogi, and an Engineer father Sh. M.A. Rastogi. Deeply inspired by both of my parents, I ended up choosing 1. to write as my passion and 2. engineering as my profession. Every word in this book is with guidance, motivation, and inspiration from my mother.

I am thankful to God for helping me gift this book to my mother. Every moment spent writing it has made me realise how I am an integral, inseparable part of her. Such is the bond of mother & daughter, where distance does not matter because as they say, *a daughter's entire life is a reflection of her mother's Aura.*

I DEDICATE THIS BOOK TO MY SOULMATE

ABHA RASTOGI

Dearest Mummy - *From you, I am.*

Contents

Preface

The moment our soul arrives on earth it gets bonded with several relations. As we open our eyes in this world, we find ourselves surrounded by the so-called blood relations of family and relatives. Though we believe that these relations are based on destiny and not by choice but there is another belief wherein it is said that the soul chooses the family based on soul's desire and expectations to be with a particular group of people and follow a particular lifestyle or to be able to effectively execute its purpose of taking birth in human form. In absence of concrete evidence and to retain a more practical approach in this book, we will limit ourselves to the boundaries of the belief that can be witnessed and believed by most of us. Having said this, we will consider blood relations or by birth relations to be those offered by destiny. We will consider other man-made relations with friends, spouses, in-laws, neighbors to be those that we choose ourselves (though destiny may have inclined us to choose them, we do hold some control in associating with them).

However, before discussing further it becomes important for us to understand the significance of relationships.

Why do relationships play such a major role in our lives?

What is the need and importance of maintaining balanced and healthy relationships?

Can we live in isolation without bothering about relationships?

It is imperative for all human beings to understand and accept the fact that our existence revolves around "WE" and not "I". And the moment, one understands the role of "WE", the significance of relationships is automatically revealed. If any of you still disagrees with the isolated individual "I", below will help clarify this further,

What is "I"?
Who am "I"?
What "I" have done?
What "I" can do?

"I" is my existence,
"I" is my individuality,
"I" am myself,
"I" am unique.

"I" am capable of doing so many tasks,
Actions that "I" did with my own hands,
Decisions that "I" took with my own brain,
"I" am responsible for all of those.
"I" am here to take its credits,
"I" am here to take its negatives.

"I" can do...

Whatever "I" want,

Whenever "I" want,

Whichever way "I" want.

"I" have full control of myself,

"I" can act, react and think,

"I" am independent.

"I" am capable.

"I" am complete.

"I" am alone.

"I" am "I".

Above is the misconception that most of us have, if not always then at some turning points of life, we often believe that "I" is all that matters. It can be during the extremely positive times when everything falls our way in a way we like when we are at peak of success and we feel we are on the top of the world, capable of independently ruling our lives as we wish. It can also happen during extremely negative times when we are in sadness, grief, or depression and opts for social isolation willingly (may be due to our hesitation to discuss our troubles or due to lack of required support from society). In such cases also, one seems to break off all the ties and start treating oneself as an individual, independent and lonely entity. This opinion of "I" being the focal point and negligence of "We" is the illusion in which we dwell during such phases of our lives. The illusion is usually developed when the mind is camouflaged with extreme success/happiness or extreme failure/sadness.

Now looking the other way round, if we consider it is always "We" that is important and not "I", then again questions crop up.

If "I" don't do anything then why am "I" praised and why am "I" blamed?

Who is there behind me controlling all these actions?

Am "I" being just a puppet, who moves the way GOD or destiny wants?

It is "GOD" who creates different circumstances, it is "GOD" who infuses different thoughts in my Mind. So, it is always "WE" together (I and GOD) who are responsible for our actions.

Now, does that mean all credit and all blame for our deeds goes to "GOD"?

If yes, how and why are we expected to improve?

This is because the human mind has the ability to control its senses, to give a direction to his/her thinking and actions. We should always remember the fact that we are supposed to make rightful efforts for our actions and leave their fruits on GOD. We should surrender all the results on the wish of GOD. Be it positive or negative. We shall just focus on our efforts to strive for following the right path.

By now, the atheist people reading this philosophy might be finding the above discussion irrelevant. Can atheist people believe in the importance of "I" alone?

The answer again will be "No". The above discussion was a broad example of our relationship with GOD and the influence of this relationship on our daily actions and decisions. However, there are other co-existing relationships, which for now we can broadly refer to as our relationship with our society which does play a significant role in framing our actions and decisions.

Always remember that –

"I" alone is incomplete
"We" completes "ME"
Sometimes "We" represent ourselves and "God",
Sometimes "We" represent our family,
Sometimes "We" represent our friends,
Sometimes "We" represent our neighbors,
Sometimes "We" represent our school/college,
Sometimes "We" represent our office,
Sometimes "We" represent our society,
Sometimes "We" represent our country,
Sometimes "We" represent our species.

And the few times when I feel that "I" represents "I", those are the times when one surrenders oneself to the attribute called "Ahankar", "Ego", "Excessive Pride" of one's actions and think that whatever appears to be done by me is actually done by me alone. The feeling which says. "I" have done this and "I" am superior to others in the crowd. However, in reality, it is not your limitless capability but the feeling of "Ego" that pulls you away from the group, away from your own people and you stand alone, firmly and rigidly neglecting the need for togetherness.

Other times when "I" represents "I" are the times of extreme "Helplessness", "Desolation", "Depression". At such times one develops a rigid belief that there is no one who can make things better. It is just "I" alone who is suffering and will keep on suffering as there can be no "We" to come to our support. Such are the times when one loses all hope and faith and at times also moves ahead with extreme steps of self-destruction or suicide.

The above insights do show us one fact that both parameters on both the extremes that push us to isolation end up with destructive results. Both feelings - the feeling of holding all powers to rule our lives alone or the feeling of being so powerless that being alone is the only option as no other can support us, drags us to social isolation, and in long run, it disrupts our normal lifestyle and needs as a human.

The moment we start heading towards social isolation, we start

Leaving behind the power of "We"...
Leaving behind the support of "We"...
Leaving behind the togetherness...
Leaving behind the belongingness...
And leaving behind the world...
That is not just built by "You" and "Me"
But by a special world called "We"... !!

The above words very clearly indicate that it is imperative for humans to have social bonding in terms of relationships. The need for mutual dependence and maintaining interpersonal relations can be minimized but never nullified. Each individual needs relationships for emotional, psychological, and social well-being. In general, no human being can survive in isolation. Everyone needs a sense of acceptance, security, love, affection, care, concern, respect, trust, faith, and all other supportive feelings from family, community, or society to deal with the challenges of life. Even the saints and hermits who seem to break all ties with the worldly relations and desires, do retain their connection with – The Creator, The Almighty, The GOD.

> ***"Man is by nature a social animal; an individual who is unsocial naturally and not accidentally is either beneath our notice or more than human. Society is something that precedes the individual. Anyone who either cannot lead the common life or is so self-sufficient as not to need to, and therefore does not partake of society, is either a beast or a GOD."***
>
> ***– Aristotle***

Acknowledgement

I would like to acknowledge my parents, Mrs. Abha Rastogi and Mr. M.A. Rastogi for being around me all the time as my anchor. They helped me sail through all the tides and struggles, I faced while writing this book.

I would like to give special thanks to my sister Nupur Rastogi, who did the first proofreading and editing of this book. She has witnessed me closely since my birth and could connect well with the theme and emotions embedded in this book. She helped me tremendously by giving valuable suggestions for shaping this book to present form.

I am blessed to get tremendous support and guidance from fellow bloggers on WordPress.

I am indebted to my writing mentor, Leigh Shulman (https://leighshulman.com), who has consistently boosted up my morale and clarified my doubts at every step.

I am obliged to my huge circle of friends and well-wishers, who always wish the best for me throughout this journey and have acted as a driving force to help me reach my destination.

Prologue

Relationships – All of us are tied to several relations/ bonds.

We all have a basic understanding of –

What are Relationships?

Why Relationships are important?

Then, why do Relationships need to be Redefined?

With redefining, this book aims to provide the in-depth essence, the embodiment of emotions, the presence of feeling which gives the true meaning to our relationship bonding.

We all grow up hearing,

"As a son, you shall do this."

"Being grandchild (even if adult), your opinion does not matter."

"Do not argue (even if it is a logical discussion) with your elders."

"As parents, it was your duty."

"No more cross-question? I am a teacher, not you."

"We take priority over your in-laws."

"Today elderly relatives are at home, you shall skip your coaching classes."

"You should have done your uncle's task before helping your neighbor."

"Your spouse is your priority now, and you have forgotten the parents who raised you up."

Even before we start speaking and understanding, we are loaded with so many relationships which are just 'name tags' for us. As we start growing up, we observe that out of nowhere, these relationship name tags are attached with a pre-defined role of conduct and expectations. It is no less than the job description of a corporate company. A long list of 'Do's and Don'ts' is taught to us. This is rightful action, as the kid at a tender age does need guidance and teachings to move forward with a disciplined lifestyle. It is important to teach about culture, society, family, and our code of conduct for them. One needs to learn the importance of offering due respect, being obedient, being patient, to be compromising, and following the norms of society.

But even after establishing so many norms, we often see conflicts in relationships. They may vary in degree-some may be open explicit conflicts and some hidden implicit conflicts. It is very common to see that someone or the other is dissatisfied with a particular relative's behavior.

Why are we not able to meet each other's expectations all the time, however hard we try?

Why do relationships become bitter?'

Why it becomes challenging to keep everyone satisfied?

Why do we regularly deal with the dilemma of prioritizing one relation over other?

The broad answer is-

Most of the time the concrete pre-defined norms make our behavior more robotic instead of a human. The rigidness in protocols, the firmness with which the flexibility is nullified make things difficult.

Brittle metals break easily than ductile metals. The hardness in brittle substances makes than easily breakable compared to flexible ductile metals.

The extrinsic teachings can work as a framework to help an individual understand the basic significance of each relationship but unless the bond is strengthened by intrinsic emotions and feelings, it doesn't become meaningful in the true sense.

This book is an effort to be able to look at each relationship with a broad mindset. To free oneself from blindly following already developed protocols and instead develop an ability to connect emotionally. To be able to do justice for each relation depending on circumstances and need of the hour, to be able to calibrate on one's role and availability, and to be able to understand that we cannot simply prioritize one relation over other like a material object.

The foundation of relations is emotional connection and not just the associated tag names connected to being a parent, child, sibling, uncle, aunt, spouse, or friend. And the foundation of emotional connection lies in the justice that we do while executing our roles and duties for each relationship with an unbiased heart.

We all find ourselves to be often entangled with priorities, expectations, complaints, and misunderstandings in the day-to-day handling of our relations. Almost none of us comes out perfect.

It is time to ponder on what can be changed to maintain harmony in all our relations, to be close to perfect (if not perfect), to be able to do justice to everyone associated with us, to develop an ability to understand and act appropriately and wisely, to avoid hurting anyone's feelings, to build a connection of trust and faith, to establish a happier and merrier surrounding.

"We were created for social connection. We are at our best when we have healthy relationships with people who genuinely care about us, respect us, and lift us up."

– Robyn L. Gobin

We shall be able to cherish the togetherness and feel blessed for all the beautiful relations and connections we have around us. The moment we feel even a pinch of burden, discomfort, or dislike being around someone or holding on or carrying a particular relationship, it is time to re-visit and analyze what's going wrong?

As always said, it is easy to break bonds but not that easy to re-establish them. So let us make an effort to move on with harmony by adopting better understanding and better emotional connection. Since any relationship is a two-way thing, it will never solely depend on one person's effort. Yet as an individual, it becomes our responsibility to do the best we can. Drop by drop, piece by piece, we can together bring some change in mindset to create a harmonious surrounding.

"Understand that you, yourself, are no more than the composite picture of all your thoughts and actions. In your relationships with others, remember the basic and critically important rule: If you want to be loved, be lovable. If you want respect, set a respectable example!"

– Denis Waitley

Chapter One

Defining Relationships

"Relationships" — The word is so long and the meaning so deep that a precise definition does not suffice its profoundness. Let's start with the dictionary meaning of Relationships,

- *the way in which two or more people or things are connected, or the state of being connected.*
- *the way in which two or more people or groups regard and behave towards each other.*

This implies that a relationship portrays a bond of connection between any two entities, it can be two-person, two groups, two communities, two countries, two objects or a person and an object and the list goes on. The way two different entities associate, connect, link, tie, bind, relate with each other show the relationship between them.

Here we will be focusing on human relationships specifically. The way two individuals are connected, the way they behave and feel for each other, the name they or society give to that bond, the unsaid expectations that come up with the name associated with that bond, the protocols one is expected to follow to maintain a healthy relationship, the challenges faced in keeping up with the expectations, and how to mitigate the issues that create misunderstandings and conflicts?

It is a vast, complex, and sensitive topic to discuss. Each individual is unique. Each individual has different habits, behaviors, upbringing, and cultural mindset. Such intrinsic (person-specific, guided by one's own nature) and extrinsic (society-specific, guided by one's family, culture, society) attributes collectively shape the unique personality of every person. This means we all may have a different way to feel and express emotions. All will have different priorities, different inclinations, and accordingly, each individual sets up different levels of expectations from each other.

A few common examples can be-

There can be two children, one who is attention-seeking, demands to pamper, expects appreciation for every little thing, and the other who is happy-go-lucky with a matured mindset and does not expect a daily demonstration of love and affection by parents.

There can be an employee who wants acknowledgment of every task done, words of appreciation for every effort, and feels demotivated if his/her manager does not satisfy his/her expectations. While there can be another employee who works hard, no matter what, feels satisfied that he/her did his best, do not change performance based on external acknowledgments but based on satisfying his/her conscious that he/her did the best.

There can be a friend who will keep on sulking if you forget to wish them on a special occasion or miss attending a special event hosted by them. While there can be others who may momentarily complain and then drop it off casually.

There can be an elderly family member, teacher, or boss who feels disrespected if your opinion differs from what they have suggested. While there can be others, who will carry on a healthy discussion and try to reach a logical, convincing, fair, and unbiased conclusion.

So, this is the world of varieties. We will have different types of relationships (family, relatives, friends, etc.) around us. Even when we share a similar relationship with multiple people (Cousins, Colleagues, Friends, Neighbours, etc.), each will have different expectations from us.

When we talk about redefining relationships, our focus is to understand them in such a way that we are able to maintain healthy and balanced relationships with almost everyone around us. Now, this is not easy but then nothing is impossible.

Why it becomes difficult to maintain healthy relationships?

Well, when we talk about relationships, the word itself makes it mandatory to have at least two people in the scene. Now two different people, connected by a common bond of relation need to balance amongst themselves to maintain a healthy and sustainable, and cherishable connection amongst them.

As it is commonly said, that we cannot clap with a single hand. The same holds true for a relationship. We cannot maintain its essence and significance one-sided. For this reason, a very common terminology of "matching frequency" is often used. If both individuals have matching frequency, which implies that both have closely similar behavior, habits, lifestyle, priorities, and a resemblance in an emotional and practical approach, they seem to agree with each other often. It becomes easy to meet each other's expectations as both follow the same approach and even without stepping in each other's shoes both will think and act almost alike. With the minimal difference in opinions, a high level of mutual understanding is developed resulting in a highly cohesive bonding.

But this is not always possible. We are associated with people of different age groups, different backgrounds, different mindsets, different priorities, different behavior, different cultures and we just can't filter everyone out of our lives for these differences. Even after being different, they may be holding an important place in our lives for some reason or other. So, it is not mandatory to keep searching for matching frequency. It is about our ability to tune up ourselves to different frequencies to enjoy healthy relations with people around us so as to happily enjoy the feeling of togetherness and harmony with our family, friends, relatives, neighbors, colleagues, and society.

Even before we take birth on this earth, we are bonded by a word called "Relationship". The first relation we are associated with is that of a Mother and Child. And the day we are born we are tied up with so many bonds, so many relations- our grandparents, parents, siblings, uncles, aunts, and a lot more. We have no control of selecting or deciding, we do not get options of validating our frequency with them, we just have one option- To learn to swim in this sea of relationships.

And there is one more relation, a unique type with the one who can't be seen by eyes, who can't be heard by ears- That's our relation with GOD.

Like newborn infants, we don't have the faintest idea of what these words mean and it is assumed that we will learn as we grow. These blood relations are implied on us not by choice but by GOD, by destiny and as we grow, we mold their meanings the way we understand, feel, or like.

There are a few relations that are based on our choice as well like friends and spouse. But we often see troubles in these too. Why? Does that mean we were not wise enough to choose the right candidate? Does that mean we are not qualified enough to choose? Or does that mean we don't really understand what to look for, what to expect?

For some of us, relationships just remain words by which we are supposed to greet each other, for some they become implied behavior that we are just supposed to follow without an escape route, for some they are duties that are to be followed too religiously in a particular, defined manner and for some, they are ***"FEELINGS WITH MEANINGS"***.

In a true sense,

Relationships are feelings with meanings.
The way we are connected has its foundation,
On the way, we feel for each other.
They are feelings to be felt,
Feelings to be enjoyed,
Feelings to be cherished,
Feelings to be expressed!!

Just attaching a tag name of a son or a brother does not suffice your relation with your parents or siblings unless your heart speaks with that love and concern for your parents and siblings.

In my perspective,

Relations are not the words
that need to be defined literally,
they are to be felt and
understood emotionally.

This is not mathematics with theorems or language with definitions. There is no measure for love, affection, care, and kindness. There is no complete definition for relations.

But there is one truth about relations. If they are pure, they are not for selfishness, they are not for your self-interest as they involve mutual acceptance on both sides. They are not for calculated give and take but they are certainly for the sharing of happiness, pleasure, and affection from both sides. They have a foundation of trust, faith, respect, understanding, compromises, and sacrifices. They are not built by force or compulsions but by feelings inside. That is why true relations are the ones that don't fade by distance for your hearts are always connected.

"We have to recognize that there cannot be relationships unless there is commitment, unless there is loyalty, unless there is love, patience, persistence."

– Cornel West

Chapter Two

Types of Relationships

Let us dive deep into this sea of relationships. Here we will focus on different types of relationships between people, how they are connected, and what does that mean? We will be exploring beyond the dictionary meaning of relation being a connection or a bond. We can understand the essence of each bond by understanding the emotions associated with these bonds. More than half of the world deals with problems in one relation or the other. So, we need to dig deep to discover the hidden meaning of this word with respect to the different types of relations that we are engaged with. We need to develop better know-how on the roots of relationships to be able to nurture them properly.

Broadly classifying, we come across two types of human connections-

1) **Explicit Relations** – These are between two individuals and can be further categorized as:
    - **By-Birth Relations** – These are the relations that automatically get linked to us the day we are born. The by-birth relations with close family (parents, siblings, etc.) are also termed as blood relations). While the by-birth relation with other people who are tied to our close family (such as relatives, friends, neighbors, and other acquaintances) can be termed as imposed relations. Depending upon an individual's nature, interests and lifestyle these imposed relations take a welcome space in one's life or can become a social obligation.
    - **Selective Relations** – These are chosen by us and mainly includes spouse, in-laws, friends, and acquaintances. Adoptions also come in this category (even though the selection primarily lies on the parental side here).
2) **Implicit Relations** – These are sort of invisible, unseen bonds. These are not between two humans. This includes our relationship with ourselves. Yes, it may sound weird but our outer self and our inner self are two different parts of our personality sharing a common bond/relation. Another example of this category is our relation with GOD. The main attribute of implicit relations is that these are entirely dependent on emotional connection and expressions. The physical expressions of love or anger by hugging or scolding are not possible here.

Let's have a closer look with a few examples,

The relation of Mother and Child

This is the first relation of a soul arriving on this earth. The relation establishes right from the day soul enters the mother's womb. This is the purest relation of all. It is engrossed with deep unconditional love, affection, trust, faith, concern, care, and the list goes on. If we look at an infant baby, it is Mom who is at the giving end. She feeds, she cares, she sacrifices, she loves, and what she gets in return – "Immense Happiness". This is the relation that starts when the child cannot speak when the child is not aware of the meaning of words spoken in his/her ears but still a crying child wants to go in mother's lap when hungry or uncomfortable.

Have you ever imagined how an infant baby understands???? Because the infant baby feels it - the love, the care, the protection, the security. Their pure heart knows what is to be felt. This means that baby and mother are emotionally connected. They do not communicate by verbal language but understand each other's needs and expectations by the emotional connection.

As children grow up, it is for them to give respect to that love and care with which they are nurtured and grown-up. Some children give it and some don't. Some listen to their heart and some listen to their matured brain which works on logic, which thinks about profit and loss, which thinks of business even in relations. Yes, here I am pointing to the two faces of children – those who spend their time and show love and affection to their aged parents; and those who see them as useless time waste and leave them alone or in senior citizen homes.

However, parents' love for children stays the same as it was unconditional, without expectations, without any self-interest. It is just that if children reciprocate by giving due respect, love, and care, it will add to the happiness of the parents and this is the least that any child can and shall do.

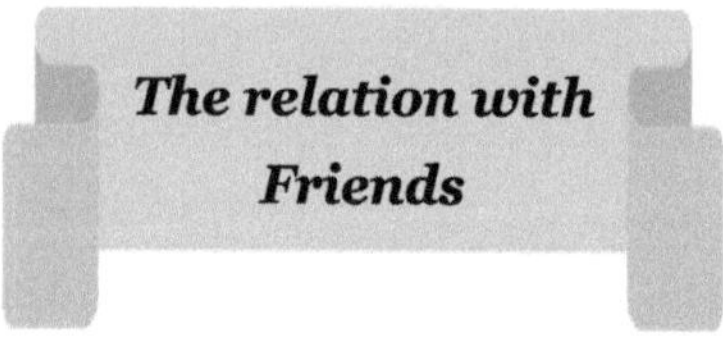

Friends are all those "***Special***" people who are not connected to us by blood relations, who are not a part of our family but still hold a very significant place and position in our lives. They are the ones who are with us in our joys and sorrows, who are with us even when they are miles apart, who care and share, who trust and understand, who encourage and motivate, who support and forgive, and whose company gives us so much joy and comfort that is beyond comparison.

"Come what may... friends will always stand your way". FRIENDS – The word is so magnificent and the relation is so *Wonderful*. You can shout at them, you can laugh

with them, you can cry with them, you can irritate them, you can eat up their time and brain, you can express all that you feel. They are the ones with whom "*You Can Be What You Are*". No formalities, no ifs, and buts, no complaints, no expectations.

The relation of our Inner Self and Outer Self

Inner Self and Outer Self are two parts of an individual's personality. The inner self is primarily guided by our soul, our subconscious mind, our heart while the outer self is dominated by rational thinking of the conscious mind and is at times manipulated.

Are we talking about Dual Personalities here?

The answer is half 'yes' and half 'no'.

The term, "dual personality" is basically used for people who present themselves in one way but they are actually feeling and thinking in some other way. It is always considered the best option to stay away from such people. These dual personalities are portrayed as those who betray, cheat or do back-biting. However, on closer look, we will realize that almost all of us have slight deviations in our inner and outer selves. As long as these deviations are harmless or meaningless to the outer world, one does not get portrayed as a dual face or non-trustworthy individual.

A quick questionnaire will help you understand this better-

- Have you ever introspected yourself?
- Do you present yourself in exactly the same manner as you are?
- How much do you know your 'own-self compared to others around you?
- How many times do you try to contradict your own thoughts?
- How many times have you felt that your subconscious is occupied by the thoughts which your conscious had shed off?
- How many times you have expressed yourself in a way that deviates from what your heart or inner voice desire because your rational thinking pushed your outer self towards a more appropriate and socially acceptable behavior?

What I can infer from above is that almost all of us have this dual personality. What we feel and how we react are not always synchronized. But in defining dual personalities we usually miss the positive aspect at times. There may be a situation when we hide our true image just because we didn't feel the need to expose it.

Does the main difference lie in identifying what actually differs in our feelings and our actions?

As long as we don't deliver any negative outcome like betraying/cheating others, we are considered clear-hearted.

There is always an "Inner Self" in us. This has always remained with you. This is something which knows all about you. Your "Actual" Self, your "True" Self. This is the "True" Self which sometimes contradicts our own decisions. This is the "True" Self that always stays in your "Subconscious" mind. But this is pure, clear, and without any biasing or fabrication.

However, our "Outer Self" is our "Presentable" self. It is manipulated at times depending on circumstances and the need of the hour. It is framed by our logical and decisive thinking, by evaluating pros and cons, by analyzing effects and results.

Now, the only thing one has to be careful about is the differences between our own Inner and Outer selves. The higher the magnitude of deviation, the higher will be the chances of conflicts within us. It results in the difference in opinion in our own decisions. The relation between our inner and outer self feels the stress with these differences and if we are unable to balance it out this becomes the root cause for disturbing our mental peace.

"Being good to yourself equates to having a positive relationship with yourself and higher self-esteem."

– Sophie Winters

So, it's time to introspect and find out if your inner-self and outer-self share a satisfactory, positive, and healthy relationship. Or do you too have a high magnitude of deviations in your inner self and outer self? Do these deviations have the potential to create imbalance and discomfort in your own feelings, decisions, and actions? Are these differences disturbing your mental peace? If yes, do work out on this and try to minimize it to the best possible extent.

Life becomes too easy and peaceful, when-
You are free,
You act the way you like,
You present the way you feel,
You talk what you want to speak,
You think and judge with your mind,
But you listen and walk with your heart!!
Always try to be what you are,
For its best...to stay the way you are!!

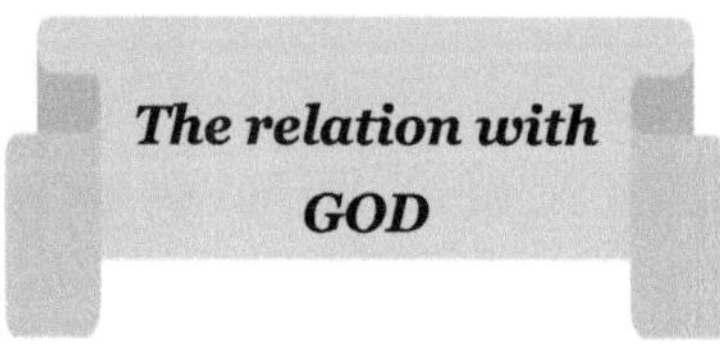

Well, this is about the relationship between GOD and ME. I was just thinking of various relationships we are bonded with. The most unique of them all is the relation between GOD and ME. To discuss its uniqueness, let me first elaborate on all other relations.

What do we expect normally in any sort of relation?

- The other person shall respect the relation the way I do.
- The other person shall express it the way I do.
- The other person shall accept it the way I do.
- The other person shall talk, think, act and feel the way I do.

But all of us are unique and have a different pattern to live life. We think differently, we act differently, and we feel different. There are some wise people who think beyond these lines and instead of binding others by their own set of rules they believe in letting the other person stay free. There are no thumb rules for expressions and feelings. There are instances where people may not appear the way you want, but that does not mean they don't respect the relationship. It is just that their ways are different.

For instance, some children stand by their parents and assure them they are with them at times of need. They give the commitment. But there are some, who do not commit anything but still, they are always there when required. So, the path is different but the end result is the same. In both cases, parents are getting the required attention and support they need.

At times people fail to accept these differences and this is where conflicts arise. Now, before starting these conflicts just spend some time observing your relation with GOD.

- We respect GOD.
- We offer our prayers to GOD.
- We talk to GOD.
- We show our dedication, commitment, trust, and belief in GOD.

Have you seen GOD?

Have you heard GOD?

Have you talked to HIM verbally (with a two-way communication), the way you talk to other people?

Do you get HIS response in the same pattern?

Does HE listen and reply to you (verbally and instantly)?

Does HE show the same dedication, commitment, trust, and belief in you?

Answer 1- "NO" and Answer 2- "YES"

It may sound absurd but I am sure our readers will have different answers to the above questions. So, we will take forward both aspects.

If your answer is "NO", you agree that GOD never communicates back. GOD does not respond to our questions. Without a direct dialogue (two-way verbal communication) between devotees and GOD, it becomes difficult to decide if GOD really has some relation with devotees or is it just an illusion?

If your answer is "YES", you agree that you can communicate with GOD but the ways are different. A devotee may not be able to see GOD but can feel GOD. GOD does not respond in the same pattern (by answering you verbally) but GOD responds. GOD listens, and answers, NOT in words, but actions. If our feelings for GOD are true and pure, GOD always responds by showing trust and belief in our intentions.

We all can now answer-

In absence of clear two-way communication, what binds devotees and GOD?

They are devotees' feelings, of course, feeling of belief, trust, and faith, feeling which tells us that GOD exists, feelings which tells us that GOD listens.

Understanding this bond of emotions will also help us in understanding and managing our explicit relations in a better manner. It is all about our perception, our feelings, our faith, our trust, and our emotional connection with that particular relation.

If the feelings are true and pure, if destiny has decided to gift you a particular relation, then cherish that bond and do your best to maintain harmony. Time does not matter; distances do not matter because it is not governed by physical proximity or availability but by heart-to-heart feelings whose proximity is not limited by physical distances.

We respect and worship GOD, and establish our relationship with GOD, which is without any boundaries even though we are not able to see GOD or talk to GOD, we can just feel GOD. This may not happen in a day, but we all know if our feelings are pure, we can feel the experience of GOD listening to us, giving answers to us, and staying with us.

Similarly, if we respect and worship all other relations in this world, with true and pure feelings we can surely break most of the barriers of misunderstandings and conflicts. We can then experience the divine happiness of being a blessed child, a blessed sibling, a blessed parent, a blessed spouse, a blessed cousin, a blessed uncle/aunt, a blessed friend, and the list go on.

Having discussed several different types of relationships around us, you all must have introspected your emotional connection with different people around you.

"You must remember, family is often born of blood, but it doesn't depend on blood. Nor is it exclusive of friendship. Family members can be your best friends, you know. And best friends, whether or not they are related to you, can be your family."

— Trenton Lee Stewart

So, expanding our vision beyond the literal meaning of relationships, we can now summarise an elaborated meaning of relationships as-

"Relationships means the sharing of feelings of love, affection, care, concern, trust, faith, respect, etc. between two persons and if one can feel it one can understand the true essence of the words called mother, father, brother, sister, husband, wife, uncle, aunts, nephews, niece, friends and above all the one and only one - Almighty GOD."

Relationships are not merely a namesake bond but a bond built with emotions and feelings embedded within it.

If Feelings Are Pure,
If Emotions Are True,
If Respect Is Real,
If Worship Is With Devotion,
If You Keep Patience,
And Destiny Is With You,
A Beautiful, Blessed Relation,
Is Surely Awaiting You...!!
May God Bless You..!!!!!!

Chapter Three

Managing Relationships

Managing all our relationships in a pleasant, harmonious, healthier manner is often a challenging task. At some point or other, with one person or another, for a valid reason or an illogical reason, we all often find it difficult to maintain balance in all of the relations, all the time.

We cannot fully control the circumstances nor the behavior, expectations, or thought processes of another related person, but we can still be vigilant, cautious, and develop a broad mindset that enables us in supporting a healthy relationship with people around us.

We will be discussing a few tips and concepts for effective handling of relations from our side.

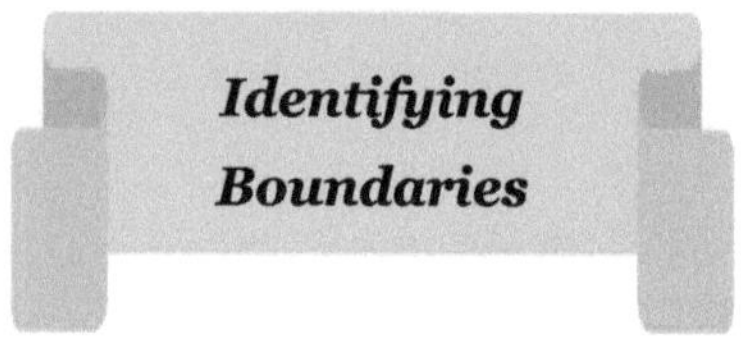

Boundary - As we all know boundary is a dividing line, a borderline that separates the two areas, a line that limits, restricts, or controls movement from one side to the other. In our daily life, we come across several such boundaries and these can broadly be classified as physical and imaginary. Physical boundaries are clearly visible to us and we all are very well aware of the fact that which ones we can cross and how?

But I want to focus here on the "Imaginary" or "Invisible" boundaries. These are the ones that we cannot see but we need to identify them by feeling them. We will discuss three types of boundaries that are significant in relationships.

1) Proximity based boundaries –

These define our degree of closeness, the extent to which we are comfortable sharing our personal space with another related person.

2) Emotion based boundaries –

These define the limitations of core emotions on which relationship is built so as to identify that the essence of core emotion is not being mitigated by bias, manipulation, or any other unreasonable motive.

3) Purpose based boundaries –

These define the extent to which we are comfortable discussing/sharing a particular purpose, decision, topic of our lives with another related person.

We will discuss these in detail with a few day-to-day life examples for better clarity.

Proximity based boundaries -

If we look at ourselves, we will realize that we have formed some boundaries around us. Our near and dear ones stand on one side of this, while strangers and acquaintances stand on the other. In fact, there are several boundaries and depending on the level of intimacy we allow people to enter those boundaries. The same goes when we deal with others. Everyone has a well-protected personal space and a defined distance that they want to maintain with a particular person.

Now having said that each person will have a set boundary for another related person, we need to understand exactly what sort of boundary is this? Is it just maintaining or feeling a particular degree of closeness in any relation or something else?

We actually need to judge this based on our relation. Since every relationship involves two people, this is mostly driven by mutual consent and acceptance. If we try to pass the undesired boundary/line of limit i.e., if we try to move closer, we may appear to be interfering in their personal space. Also, if we try to maintain too much distance, it seems we don't respect the other person's closeness to us. In short, if we don't identify the limits in a justified and desired manner, or if both related people do not agree, accept and respect each other's boundaries, then conflicts may arise. The challenge is to identify each other's boundaries and stay within those limits – neither near nor far. So boundary as we understand here is one's personal space. We will discuss this further under the concept 'Live and Let Live'.

Emotion based boundaries-

As we have already discussed, the foundation of relationships lies in a group of emotions and feelings attached. So when we are talking about relationship boundaries, this in fact implies the degree or magnitude of embedded emotion on which that relationship is built. These can be care, concern, trust, faith, love, belief, and so on. Even though these are unmeasurable entities but still we tend to assign some degree or conditions to these to define their amplitude or significance in a particular relation.

A few examples can be –

You can trust your colleague for the travel and tourism advice but you may not be able to trust the same person for the best professional advice (as an office is a place where you both are competitors).

You might feel blessed to receive immense love and care from your grandparents but at times they become overprotective and may hinder your professional growth. Like when they come to know that you will be moving to a prestigious college abroad, they try to influence you to drop the idea of leaving your hometown.

Your younger sibling is very close and affectionate. You have always pampered him/her and met all the expectations and demands happily. But when that younger sibling starts expecting unfair favor from you like raising unreasonable demands for expensive, luxurious gifts or recommending him for a job that he/she does not deserve but your recommendation can help them, then meeting such expectations does not sound correct.

Biased behavior is very commonly seen and felt in every relation and it can be for our welfare or vice-versa. Yes, we all live in a world where the strength of relationships is defined by – blind trust, blind faith, blind love, but sometimes we end up paying a heavy cost for this blindness.

These are one of the most difficult of all boundaries. Such boundaries which if not identified may land us in big trouble.

How to identify the faint boundary line between the following extremes (where one side of the line is good and the other is not)?

Trust is Good... Blind Trust is not...

Faith is Good... Blind Faith is not...

Caring is good...Over-protection is not...

Showing concern is good... Interfering is not...

But how can one draw a boundary line between the above? They are so near, yet so far. The only answer to this lies in your own intrinsic ability to be able to balance out your emotional connection and your rational thinking in such a way that you can wisely notice and adhere to such distinction lines.

We need to visualize each and every instance with an unbiased mindset, we need to draw a boundary for instances where the core emotion starts getting trapped in the clouds of confusion, where we start feeling the disconnect or discomfort. It is always advised to discuss such decisions with another person who can give more rational suggestions.

Remember-

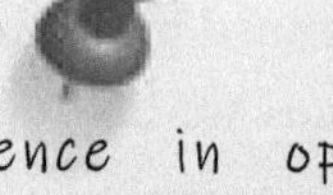

The difference in opinions does not mean disrespecting relations.

Disagreements do not mean that your emotional connection is weak.

There is nothing wrong in listening to all but doing what your heart yearns for.

There is nothing wrong with reaching out to another person for an unbiased opinion.

Just because your thoughts and decisions differ for a particular thing does not mean that your relationship is not strong, or the closeness of your bond is getting altered.

Purpose based boundaries

This revolves around the fact that we all chose different people around us to discuss or confide in different topics/matters of our lives.

You may have one person with whom you are comfortable discussing your profession, some other for discussing your health, some other for discussing finances, and some other for just chilling out or shopping or traveling.

We all can relate to the Airtel Advertisement lines here,

Chai ke liye jaise toast hota hai
Vaise har ek friend zaroori hota hai
Aise har ek friend zaroori hota hai
Koi subah paanch baje neend se jagaye
Koi raat ko teen baje jaan bachaye
Ek teri kadki mein sharing kare
Aur tere budget mein sneak in kare
Koi nature se guest koi host hota hai
Par har ek friend zaroori hota hai
Ek ghadi ghadi kaam aaye par kabhi kabhi call kare
Ek kabhi kabhi kaam aaye aur ghadi ghadi call kare
Gossip ka koi ghoomta phirta satellite
Koi sath rahe toh kar de sab alright
Koi effortless koi forced hota hai
Lekin har ek friend zaroori hota hai
Chatroom friend koi classroom friend

Koi bike pe race wala vroom vroom friend
Shopping mall wala shopping friend
Exam hall wala copying friend
Movie buddy groovie buddy
Hi buddy.... bye buddy
Joke buddy poke buddy
Gaana buddy shaana buddy
Chaddi buddy yaar buddy
Everybody... sab buddy
Par har ek friend zaroori hota hai
Lekin har ek friend zaroori hota hai
Har Friend Zaroori hai, yaar!

– Amitabh Bhattacharya

Thus what aspects or concerns of one's life one wants to share with other people varies. There is a boundary line for topics we freely communicate about. If you have two friends, and you are comfortable discussing your financial things with one, it does not mean that other friends do not hold any value. Neither, another friend shall forcefully try to invade your territory on topics that you do not want to discuss with them. Respecting each other's comfort zone for various matters of discussion will avoid instances of bitterness and conflict in relationships.

> *"Boundaries in relationships can be much more difficult to create and honor. And if its a boundary that someone does not inherently wants or understands - then there maybe huge problems because that boundary can just be crossed again and again."*
>
> *– Dr. Margaret Rutherford*

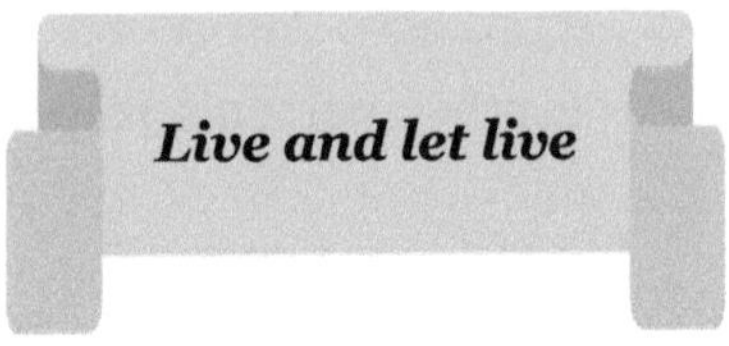

A small simple phrase yet so powerful – "Live and Let Live".

Just think of the instances, when people around you poke their nose and try to interfere in your life. I think most of us have such interfering people around us and some of them must be here reading this. Now, they will have the justification that we don't interfere, we care. But always remember that - "Unsolicited advice is never welcomed or respected".

The boundaries concept discussed above clearly outlines that we all have our "personal boundaries". These boundaries vary for different people and if anyone seems to intervene or cross the boundary line we have set for them, we feel irritated and disturbed and maybe angry too. One shall always remember that if other people consider you worthy enough to share their views with, they will do it themselves. Always keep this in mind while communicating. If you are discussing a topic or asking a question, to which the other person seems hesitant to respond, then do not keep on probing further. Do understand that they are uncomfortable and stop right there. The only exception can be cases where a person is hesitant, not due to boundary intervention but because they never know they can confide in you and open up discussion on a particular topic. So observe carefully and wisely and react accordingly. Always remember to stay away whenever the other person's response seems to convey that – it's none of your concern! Lots of conflicts and misunderstandings can be avoided if we all can understand this and respect each other's personal space.

"Don't explain your feelings. They belong to you."

– Paulo Coelho

Understanding Misunderstandings

MISUNDERSTANDING – The root cause of several conflicts, disputes, disassociations, and break-ups.

It is a human tendency to judge people based on their actions. We observe, judge, and frame some opinions about everyone around us. In the process, we sometimes end up with a wrong interpretation also. We shall remember that neither we nor our observations are always perfect. At times what we see or perceive is not what is reality. There may be different circumstances and reasons for a person to behave in a particular manner. What matters are the intentions!

The only way to tackle such misunderstandings is to validate your assumptions and perceptions. The best way could be to openly discuss and communicate your assumptions, confusions, or interpretations, and allow another person to present his/her viewpoint/ clarifications. But some people become so egoistic, so self-obsessed, so angry or so confident that they prefer ending up the things instead of moving forward with an effort to resolve.

"There is nothing more dreadful than the habit of doubt. Doubt separates people. It is a poison that disintegrates friendships and breaks up pleasant relations. It is a thorn that irritates and hurts; it is a sword that kills."

– Gautama Buddha

So, if you seem to have a good and healthy cohesive relation with someone, that is now moving towards the unhealthy side then don't frame any opinions or take any actions impulsively.

> ***"Assumptions are the termites of relationships."***
>
> ***— Henry Winkler***

Before framing any rigid opinion, one shall listen to instincts, one shall evaluate the past records, one shall always give a second thought, one shall always analyze how trustworthy and faithful the other person was, and above all one shall try for open communication and not just believe on self-framed opinions. No one can change in a day.

Instead of deriving a conclusion about the other person being changed, think over it and find out if it is just a misunderstanding? Also do not take it a long way.

'It is always difficult to heal old wounds.'

So never let the discomfort or bitterness in your relationships grow to an extent from where comeback becomes difficult or impossible. The moment you notice that misunderstanding is cropping in between, move forward and evaluate the ongoing circumstances. While doing so do not limit yourself to things that you both share but also the circumstances that one is dealing with at an individual's end.

For example, your friend who has always shared your happiness wholeheartedly now avoids attending your birthday party or promotion party or even wedding. Though nothing has changed between both of you, on the personal front, your friend is disturbed. It could be due to loss of job, health issue/chronic disease diagnosis of a family member, or some other family or property disputes due to which he/she always feels stressed.

It is better to cut the roots of such misunderstandings before they become too firm and you end up building a big boundary line of bitter relationship on its foundation.

Relationships are too precious; don't just let them fade away for mere misunderstanding.

But again, there is a word of caution. There are two faces of every coin. When we say our perception or interpretation or understanding can be wrong at times, it means that it can be wrong at any phase.

It may also happen that the one who we trust was never worth trusting. Sometimes, we have people around us who appear close and sweet as they need some favor from us. The moment they realize they no longer need us, they show their true colors.

It may also happen that due to certain experiences, the person has really changed. Sometimes, one experience some extreme situations. It can be on the positive side like winning a jackpot or cracking a tough exam. It can be on the negative side like being betrayed by a close friend or family member, losing someone close (grief). Such extreme circumstances abruptly create a Tsunami of emotions and sometimes the person becomes so overwhelmed with such extreme experiences that their behavior and personality change drastically. This may settle down after a brief time period or this may change them forever. Now it is on us, to understand the genuineness of change and accept them with a changed attitude (usually, this is recommended when a person changes due to negative situations in life) or to maintain distance in that relation until the past behavior is restored (even if it means that this distance may gradually end up the relation).

It may also happen that the person does not find you as worthy as before. Sometimes (especially in friendships) it is observed that two people are very close but then the entry of a third new member impacts the closeness of the other two. At any point in time, one may find another friend with whom they tune better and, in such cases, people start ignoring the old friend.

It may happen that when something objectionable and alarming happened, we ignored it thinking it's just a misunderstanding. It may also happen that when you approached for clarifications you were misguided. So when we talk about MISUNDERSTANDINGS, it is very important to understand that it actually pertains to visualization and interpretation of circumstances based on facts and not on assumptions, based on justice and not on bias. Merely ignoring a fact considering it as 'misunderstanding' can be troublesome. There are people with dual faces, they look sweet and they attack you from the back. One needs to be alert with such people. In fact, sometimes such experiences make us see everyone around us with doubt and suspicion.

With all this said, I would like to conclude that-

Listen to your mind,
Listen to your heart,
Listen to your instincts.
Watch the actions,
Frame the observations.
Do the analysis,
Try to find out...
What is CHANGING?
If it is the person?
Or the circumstances?
Is it a correct interpretation?
Or mere misunderstanding?
Don't over-react,
Track the past records.
But be vigilant,
Don't just ignore,
If such instances repeat.
Be balanced...
Be Calm...
Be patient.
And just move forward,
With what pleases you the most.

It is like a complex puzzle without a defined thumb rule. One needs to collectively apply one's rational thinking, analysis, emotional understanding, instincts and accordingly move forward with a suitable and appropriate action.

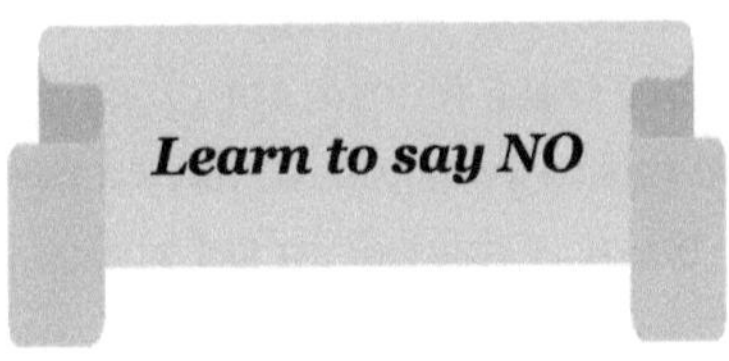

No, No, No...
How can I say "NO"?
How can I refuse?
How can I deny it?
How can I object?
How can I oppose?

We have different circumstances, different reasons, different places where we feel the urge to say "NO", but we just cannot.

Starting with office, how difficult it is for you to say "NO" :

- When you have a target in front of you and a team member asks for leave.
- When you are overloaded with work one after other in parallel.
- When you are allocated work that is not supposed to be done by you.
- When you are expected to do favors that are not recommended professionally.
- When you are instructed to leave aside your important personal commitments and assignments repetitively, for the sake of achieving unrealistic professional deadlines.

People avoid saying "NO", thinking that it will ruin their performance track record, appraisal, and reputation. It is good to be fair to your job, to have a positive attitude towards work but it is not fair to get yourself exploited.

Coming on the personal front, how difficult it is for you to say "NO" :

- When you have to lend your vehicle at the time when you also need it.
- When you have to lend money for luxuries at the time when you need it for your necessities.
- When you go out shopping or to watch a movie against your will.
- When you are ready to do things against your will just because that is what your family/friends want you to do.

People avoid saying "NO", thinking that it may disappoint/hurt the other person. Again, it is good to be concerned and to respect each other's feelings but not to the extent that it becomes a burden/pressure/inconvenience for us. This means going against your wishes to respect another person's opinion or interests is perfectly fine but only when you are able to do so wholeheartedly without holding any grudges or discomfort within you for being forcefully and unwillingly pulled up into that decision or activity.

Saying "NO" is often difficult for some people as they consider it to be a rude behavior trait. But always saying 'YES' against your wishes and carrying a baggage of discomfort is also not recommended. Also, it is not necessary that other people will always feel bad about listening to your "NO". Sometimes the other person is simply unaware of the fact that they are dragging you into something that you don't like or are not comfortable doing at the moment or that you have another task in hand that holds more priority. So, it is more about being transparent in communication. We shall always decide some priorities, maintain some criteria, and make some boundaries so that we don't land up losing our own mental peace. Remember that transparent and open communication and expression are also a foundation stone of a healthy relation.

Your forceful "YES" may turn out to be more harmful than your straightforward "NO".

Again, I will suggest that it cannot be applied everywhere as a concrete thumb rule. One needs to take a wise decision on a case-to-case basis. At some places forceful "YES" could be the best approach while at others a straightforward "NO" could be the best approach.

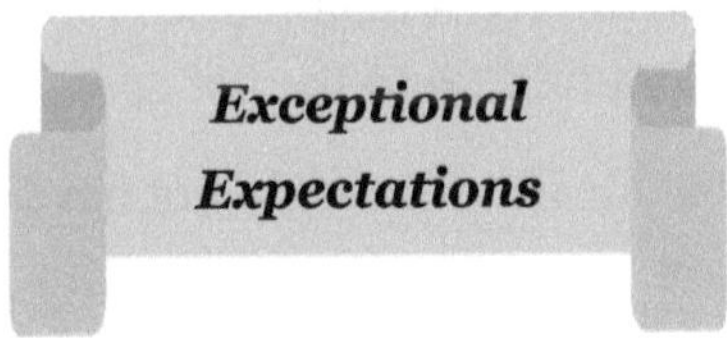

"Expectations" – We all are familiar with this and almost all of us are connected with this word. Expectations are strong belief and hope of achieving or receiving something material or immaterial. There can be expectations for well-being, good health, money, success, love, care, respect, etc. Expectations do play an important role in relationships as every relation has some expectations attached to it. Every relationship revolves around two types of expectations-

- ***'Our Expectations'*** from ourselves, from others, from society, from God.
- ***'Expectations Of Others'*** (family, friends, society, God, etc.) from us.

There are different levels, different platforms, and different viewpoints for these expectations, but the absence of "expectations" is the rarest of rare. In fact, a closer look will show that no one is entirely free from expectations. If it is not from others, it is from self or from GOD. It is almost impossible for any human being to live without any expectation. So expectations always exist within each one of us.

Seems like the above lines have triggered your brain. So, what are you thinking? How true it is?

I too have expectations from self, from family, from friends, from office, from neighbors, from society, from government, from GOD, and the list goes on and on.

It is said that ideally, we should not have expectations. The more you expect, the more you suffer from disappointment.

"When you stop expecting people to be perfect, you can like them for who they are."

– Donald Miller

But are we able to accept these ideologies practically?

Is it wrong?

- To expect care, concern, and love from family.
- To expect help, trust, and understanding from friends.
- To expect coordination, cooperation, and support from colleagues.
- To expect respect, recognition, and justice in office.
- To expect good infrastructure, law, and order from the government.
- To expect good and hygienic food in restaurants.
- To expect reliable products from shopkeepers.
- To expect good services as a customer.
- To expect the best for yourself.
- To expect blessings from GOD.

And, here comes the twist.

What are our Expectations?

What are our Aspirations?

What do we Deserve?

What is our Right?

We often mix and use all of these interchangeably. We broadly consider our dreams or aspirations, our rights, and the results of what we deserve, under a common umbrella of 'Expectations'. Yes, these can be termed as our expectations but when we talk about what we deserve and what is our right, both have realistic boundaries. Their levels can be clearly defined.

- If you have written all your answers correctly, you deserve good marks.
- If you have delivered the required output, you deserve committed compensation/salary.
- If you pay your taxes on time, you have the right to get better infrastructure.
- If you pay in a restaurant/shop, you have to right to claim the quality and reliability of the product received.

But what we expect, what are our ambitions/ aspirations, do not have any pre-defined limits. At times we set these limits as per our desires and at times there are no boundaries at all. They are spread across a vast range. They totally depend on us. Our thinking, our efforts, and our understanding.

If you performed well in your examinations and expect to be the class topper, it is a limit set by you. You don't deserve it unless there are none of the other students who have performed better than you.

If you did your best in the office, you expect an X% increment. Again, a limit is set by you. You deserve the best increment, but it may be less, equal, or more than X%.

If you expect care and love from family, trust of friends, coordination from colleagues, it is just your wish, your limit. It is not necessary that what we expect is what they will give. They will give as per their wish, their limits. Even though, a very common belief is, "***You Reap What You Sow.***" By applying this concept to relationships, we start expecting that our behavior, our expressions of love, care, concern, respect, kindness, etc., our prioritization or value for a particular relationship will be reciprocated similarly and equally. But this is not always true. In that case, shall we alter our behavior as well?

"Treat people how you want to be treated instead of how they treat you."

– Kristin Michelle Elizabeth

It is up to us to decide on the levels of expectations from others, but we cannot control beyond this decision. Even after doing our best and setting a good example from our side, we need to be well aware of the fact, that we can set our limits but we cannot define/guide others. They will behave the way they want. They may be a priority for us and we may be ready to spend a lot of our time with them. But for them, something else could be a priority. The concept of time is also highlighted here because this comes up as a very common reason for several relationship conflicts. It is assumed and expected that one will spend more time with the person one values most. When these expectations are not met, conflicts crop up. So whenever actions, expressions, and availability of other related people do not synchronize with our expectation levels, we start cribbing.

Is it right? Are we authorized to speak for the limits of other people?

The answer is – "NO".

Do your best. Do what satisfies you. But not with the feeling of expecting the same in return but with the feeling of satisfying your own conscious. If we can follow this concept, we can minimize several day-to-day conflicts in our relationships with others.

> ***"I do my thing and you do your thing. I am not in this world to live up to your expectations, and you are not in this world to live up to mine. You are you, and I am I. And if by chance we find each other, it's beautiful."***
>
> ***– Fritz Perls***

As discussed earlier, relationships are not built upon calculated give and take. It is more about sharing and exchanging and the quantity and quality may not always reciprocate proportionately. This means if as a sibling you are showering all your love and care it does not mean that it will always be reflected back to you in the same proportion or same manner. So, if the behavior or expression exhibited by you comes up with the expectation of receiving it back, then things may not always fall your way.

However, if it is unconditional, without any expectations then whatever comes back is a pleasure and there are no grudges for what does not come back. It sounds like a very idealistic approach and I agree it is not easy to follow it practically. However, we can follow it to a certain extent, that is by keeping our expectations as low as possible (if not zero).

Relationships do need compromise, understanding, flexibility, and adjustment. If we can equalize,

What we expect from another person	=	**What other person can comfortably give**

That is if we make an effort to adjust our expectation limits to a more feasible and comfortable target keeping in view the capacity and initiative of another person, then things settle down well.

Setting up exceptionally high standards of our expectations only ends up making our life a mess full of complaints, dissatisfaction, and disappointment. But having no expectation at all may also end up with people taking our advantage. It is up to us to clearly define the limits of these expectations. In my view, they shall neither be exceptionally low nor exceptionally high.

Expectations with low limits take us to exploitation.

Expectations with justified limits take us to satisfaction.

Expectations with high limits take us to frustration.

These limits are in our own hands,
We are the ones who set them.
And we are the ones who choose
To be exploited, satisfied, frustrated.
So, choose your limit,
And choose your happiness,
It's there...
Within YOU.

"Keeping up with low expectations,helps to maintain healthier relationships."

Chapter Four

Wanted vs Unwanted Relationships

There are certain relationships that we enjoy and others that we just carry on for namesake. It is not just limited to relationships by birth but applies to all relationships that we get associated with as we grow – relations with family, relatives, schoolmates, neighbors, workplace colleagues, and even the acquaintances of your close family (your grandparents, parents), their native place neighborhood, etc. In a vast community, even a small child will find himself/herself surrounded by so many relations that at times it becomes confusing, and appears like a compulsive burden. As all relationships come with a set of protocols that shall be followed, dealing with multiple related people simultaneously becomes challenging. As we grow, we start developing our own likes and dislikes and do not always feel comfortable in the company of everyone associated with us. Besides these by-birth associations, there are several other instances where one association will link you with several relations.

The most common example is that of a marriage. It is not just your spouse and parents-in-law but each and every relation of your spouse that comes to you as a mandatory attachment. It will be your spouse's extended family, relatives, friends, neighbors, acquaintances – you will be linked to all. They all become part of your relationship world. Others can be the institutions that we associate with – school, office, residential society, etc. If you are a student, you are bound to respect each and every staff/teacher that are part of that school. You are expected to maintain amicable relations with all other students. Though this is mostly violated as students do show up their grudges but then this is their unexpected behavior and they are consistently guided to maintain harmony despite differences and dislikes. If you are an employee, you are bound to respect your juniors, peers, and seniors and maintain professional decorum (even if you dislike someone there for some reason, you cannot explicitly express that). If we are part of a particular system or institution, we are supposed to maintain harmony (even if it's just a courteous relation of an acquaintance).

So amongst all the relations around us, there are a few that we are ready to follow wholeheartedly while others are just attached to us for namesake. Broadly classifying,

1) **Wanted Relationships** - These relationships are the ones that have understanding, care, concern, respect, trust, faith and are maintained with goodwill. In these, the person feels comfortable, secure, and pleasant, and often cherishes the company of people associated. At times, the relation might not be on the positive extreme means a person may not be very much fond of that relation, but still, it is considered wanted as long as it is balanced. This means, if it is sure that one does not feel sick or uncomfortable in carrying a particular relation, then that relation has due acceptance and falls in the category of wanted relationship. These are ***Harmonious Relationships***, well managed, easy to carry, and often work as a support system for you.

2) **Unwanted Relationships** - These relationships have disagreements, bitterness, discomfort, jealousy, insecurity, and negative vibes. At times it is possible to break up and let go of such relations but it is not always possible. For instance, if you have an unhealthy relationship with a close relative, in-laws, sibling, or someone in your college/neighborhood/workplace, etc., you cannot always have the option of distancing yourself forever. For general courtesy and societal image, we often pretend to maintain that relation artificially. The closer the person is, the difficult it becomes to pretend. Also, there is a possibility that over a period of time the bitterness reaches an extent of toxicity. This means that forcefully carrying on with such a relation, or being around such an unwanted person starts affecting

your mental peace thus disturbing your emotional balance and also impacting your overall well-being. These are ***Toxic Relationships***, difficult to manage, and often interrupts one's mental peace. Depending on the level of toxicity and an individual's tolerance level, it becomes necessary to distance oneself (to the extent possible) before it starts showing its impact on your emotional and physical well-being. However, before distancing one needs to properly evaluate that the bitterness is not a result of improper communication or misunderstanding. At times a common contact can also work as a mediator and try to sort out the differences and conflicts. So, depending on the circumstances, one shall work out all possible options to maintain the connection and shall opt for distancing only as the last resort.

Let's have a closer look at how people react and feel in a wanted vs unwanted relation. As the above discussion has clearly distinguished these as harmonious and toxic relationships, we will be using this terminology henceforth with some examples to have a better grip on emotions embedded within these, how they are expressed, or how one usually acts and react in these.

Wanted/Harmonious Relationships -

"Harmonious Relationships focus on celebrating togetherness and results in attractive bonding."

We are well aware of the dedicated ways of celebrating relationships such as Mother's Day, Father's Day, Valentine's Day, Friendship Day, Children's Day, Raksha Bandhan (Indian festival signifying brother-sister bond), Karwachauth (Indian festival signifying husband-wife bond), Thanksgiving day, etc. The list is not limited as the internet is showing me grandparents' day, siblings' day, and many more. All of these celebrations revolve around celebrating the joy and happiness associated with the bond of a pleasant relation. Though, in this age of social media and with the world gripped by societal image, it is not correct to infer that anyone who celebrates Mother's Day also gives that respect and love to his/her Mom that she deserves. Also, I am of the opinion that such bonds cannot be limited to a single-day celebration but deserves a lifelong celebration. But the mere existence of such occasions (most of which are celebrated worldwide), do signify that these relationships hold a precious space in our lives and deserve celebrations.

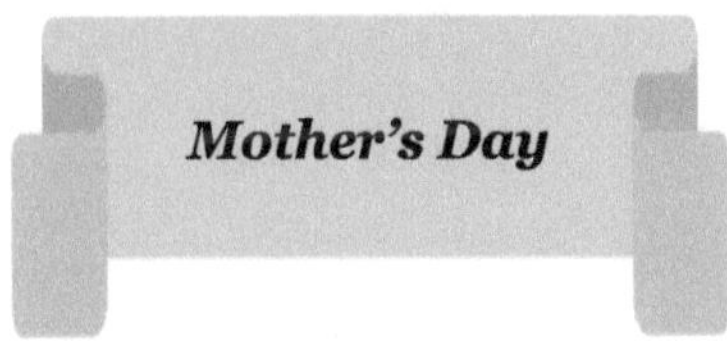

Mother's Day is celebrated on the second Sunday of every May.

Mummy, Mumma, Mom, Mother - The first relationship with which a child gets bonding. The first feeling that a child feels – the feeling of belongingness, the feeling of togetherness. The everlasting bond is built on the foundation of love and faith. A mother's love and affection for a child is beyond compare. It is the purest relations of all. The mother holds a sweet, special, wonderful, bond with children.

We don't have words to define,
We don't have sentences to explain,
For what we have are feelings,
Which are to be expressed.
What we have is love,
Which cannot be measured.
But you know and we know,
Child and Mother is a bond,
Where the unsaid is understood.
And, you know and we know,
That between us,
Infinite unconditional LOVE flow.

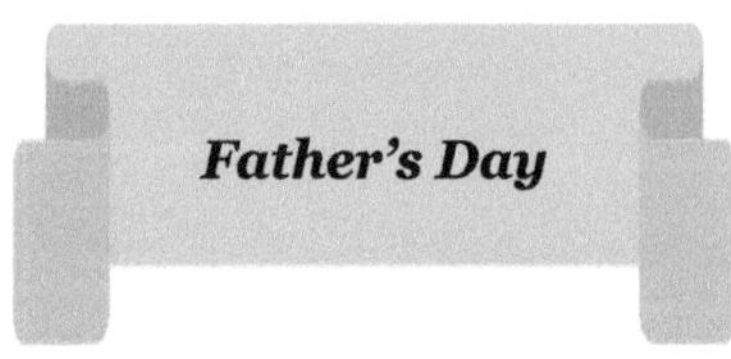

Father's Day is celebrated on the third Sunday of every June.

Father, Papa, Dad, Daddy – For every child this word holds a special feeling of support, guidance, love, and care. He is the one who teaches us how to walk, how to run, and how to live in this world? When Mom teaches us about emotions, sentiments, and feelings, Father teaches us about practicality and reality. He gives us the vision to differentiate between right and wrong. He guides us on how to face this world, how to accept the truth, how to cope up with problems, and how to stay strong? He seems to be tough but is soft actually; he seems to be practical but is emotional too.

Here, in actual the role of father and mother both are significant as a parent and my description above does not imply that what a mother teaches, a father cannot or vice versa. It is just that both Mother and Father groom up the child in their own different ways and hold a very special place as a parent in a child's world.

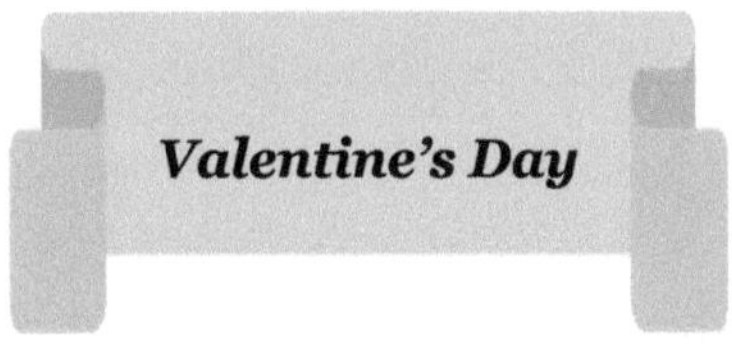

Valentine's Day is celebrated on the 14th of February every year.

The origin of this day lies with great St. Valentine sacrificing his life for the sake of others. The history and origin of "Valentine's Day" are not clear as there are different legends associated with different parts of the world and different phases of time. But, one instance that can be evidenced at several places is that *'St. Valentine was a priest in Rome. When Roman Emperor decided that single men made better soldiers than those with wives and families, St. Valentine stood against this injustice. He performed marriages of these young soldiers. But his actions were discovered by Emperor and he was put to death.'*

'St. Valentine sacrificed his life for his love to humanity.'

Now it is on us, how to respect and how to celebrate this day, as it is not just an epitome of love for your sweetheart. In many countries, a trend has started to communicate the feeling of love to a parent, a child, a sibling, or a friend on Valentine's Day. Everyone needs to be loved, and often many relationships are taken for granted, but on Valentine's Day, each one of us can make an extra effort to express these emotions in a special way.

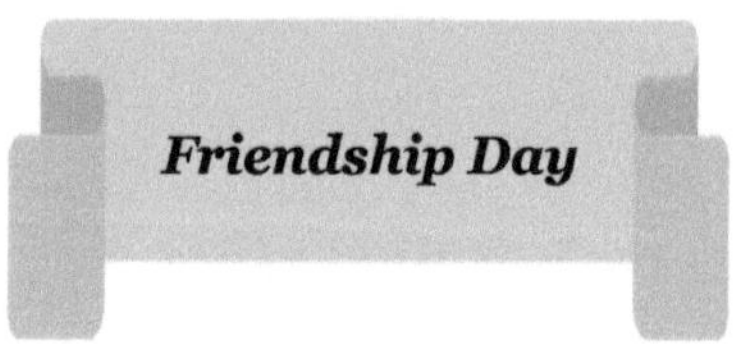

Friendship Day

Friendship Day is celebrated on the first Sunday of every August.

Friendship—It is one of the most beautiful and amazing relationships.

Friendship...

Where you are what you are,
Where you do what you want,
Where you talk about what you feel,
And where you act the way you like.

Friendship...

Where you give and take,
Without any expectations,
Without any compulsions,
Without any questions,
And without any reasons.

Friendship...

Where there are no formalities,
No excuses,
No complaints,
No explanations.

Friendship...

Where you may be miles apart,
Where you may not talk for months,
But when you talk, when you meet,
It seems like you were never away.

Friendship...

Where you feel happy,
To see others happy,
And where you are ready to do anything,
To make the other happy.

Friendship...

The first place where you knock,
When in need or trouble,
The first person you rely on,
In your difficult times.

Friendship...

Where all you have is Trust,
Faith,
Belief,
And Confidence in each other.

Friendship...

A bond forever,
A bond so cherishable,
A bond worth praising,
A bond so amazing.

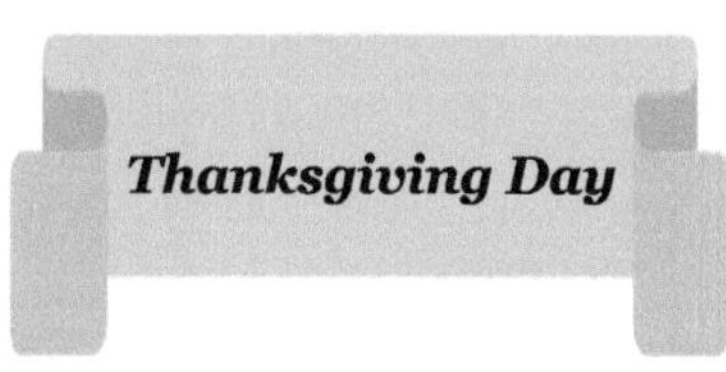

Thanksgiving Day is celebrated on the fourth Thursday of every November.

“Thank you” is the most common and globally used way of expressing gratitude. Dictionary meaning defines *“THANKS” as*:

‘a polite expression used when acknowledging a gift, service, or compliment, or accepting or refusing an offer.’

Well, if we look back for the past few days, a few months, or rather a few years and think of instances, where we really felt the “urge” to say “Thank you”, we will get a clearer picture. We utter “Thank you” when someone opens the door for us, when someone halts the lift for us, when shopkeeper hands over goods, conversation on phone for some official purpose when some stranger helps/co-operates and the list goes on.

But how often do we THANK our close ones?

Our Mom who cares for us day and night, our parents/grandparents/spouse who cooks delicious food for us every day, our father who guides us on each and every step in this walk of life, our siblings who share all our joys and sorrows, and our best friends who stand by us come what may.

How many times do we utter “Thank you”?

How many times do we give them a “Thank you” note?

These are the people who have touched our life, who have made our life worthy and joyful, who have made us feel special, who have given us a feeling that is priceless and beyond comparison. For these people, “Thank You” at times seems to be too small and too formal.

But still, it feels great to express gratitude to these "Very Special" people around us. Even though they all don't need words to describe their value, they do not expect any sort of Thanks from us because what they do for us is unconditional and without any expectation. In fact, they usually don't need the expression or acknowledgment of our gratitude in words as they are too close to read it in our eyes.

So here, let us list down a few cherishable moments, that bring a smile on our face, happiness in our heart, and of course the pleasure of having such "special relations" in our life:

I love the way you care,

I love the way you share,

I love the way you understand,

I love the way you guide,

I love the way you motivate,

I love the way you inspire,

I love the thoughtful discussions we share,

I love the way you trust me,

I love the way you celebrate my happiness,

I love the way you encourage,

I love the way you appreciate,

I love the way you divide my sorrows,

I love the way you stand by in tough times,

I love the way you show concern,

I love the way you convince,

I love the way you forgive,

I love the way you support,

I love the way you are always there,

Even if we are miles apart,

And the frequency of communication is rare.

How can I just say "THANK YOU" for all of the above?

But I want to show my gratitude by letting you know that:

"I Feel Blessed To Have You In My Life!!

You Are A Precious Treasure!!

A Valuable Possession!!

And A Cherishable Relation!!"

By now, the reminders of beautiful ways of celebrating the togetherness of our precious relationships must have fuelled you with new energy. Each one of us can connect and relate with some of the expressions and emotions and feelings portrayed in the above relationship celebrations. The joy and harmony that such relations give us, fill us with positive vibes and work as an accelerator in promoting our emotional well-being which in turn makes us satisfied, successful, pleasing, and attractive personalities.

Unwanted/Toxic Relationships -

The biggest challenge of Toxic Relationships is identification and acceptance. It is always advised to handle bitter or unhealthy relationships with extreme care. They become as fragile as a glass which is very easy to break but impossible to fix back. So, it becomes mandatory to rule out all the possibilities of misunderstanding, compromise, and patch up, before considering any relationship to be entirely toxic and not worth carrying further. One shall also work out in detail the pros and cons of carrying it on with set boundaries and distancing or carrying it with a little compromise on one's expectations. Toxicity can be of different forms. It can be jealousy, cruelty, superiority complex, inferiority complex, lack of mutual understanding, frequent disagreements, or simply rejection/neglect making you feel unwanted or non-existent in another person's life.

"Indifference and neglect often do much more damage than outright dislike."

– J.K. Rowling

As relation is a two-way bond, if you feel totally neglected and rejected and it induces sadness and pain, and the other person is not ready to give you the required worth, it's time to stop running behind with hope. Either lower your expectations and accept to continue that bond keeping a distance but if it gives you pain, do disassociate.

> ***"The person you're meant to be with will never have to be chased, begged or given an ultimatum."***
>
> ***– Mandy Hale***

There is always a dilemma when we deal with such Toxic Relationships. Sometimes we may feel that we are over-reacting, it's a misunderstanding, it's circumstantial, it's manageable. Sometimes we may feel that we are bound to carry on a particular bond for the societal image. Sometimes we are not ready to accept that relationship is toxic, we just keep convincing ourselves that it is not how it looks. Sometimes we become too impulsive and decide to break away the ties. Whatever we do, we always keep questioning ourselves if we did right or wrong?

The major approach for dealing with bitter or unpleasant relationships and concluding them as Toxic Relationships will primarily need below steps,

- **Identify** (rule out the possibility of misunderstanding)
- **Accept** (do not stay hopeful of resolving the bitterness, if you have done all possible effort)
- **Compromise** (lower your expectations and learn to live with it with present conditions without disturbing your mental peace by feeling sad again and again about the bitterness in relation)
- **Break Up** (distance or free oneself from that relation forever prioritizing your well-being, if a compromise is not helping).

> ***"It hurts to let go. Sometimes it seems the harder you try to hold on to something or someone the more it wants to get away. You feel like some kind of criminal for having felt, for having wanted. For having wanted to be wanted. It confuses you, because you think that your feelings were wrong and it makes you feel so small because it's so hard to keep it inside when you let it out and it doesn't come back. You're left so alone that you can't explain."***
>
> ***– Henry Rollins***

Let's discuss further managing unpleasant relationships. Some relationships are always uncomfortable for us (the namesake relations). But some have been pleasant and then start taking an unpleasant turn. We will discuss a few concepts which will help us understand better regarding the bitterness or discomfort cropping up in an otherwise pleasant relation, and how to tackle it.

Trrinnnn Trrinnnn ... Beep Beep... Blink Blink...

Hope this is what comes to your mind when you hear about Alarms.

Wake Up Alarms, Fire Alarms, Emergency Alarms are one of those few alarms which alert us when we listen/see them. We then either respond to them or ignore them. And we all know ignoring them may get us in trouble. These troubles can be minor such as getting late at the office/college, missing train or flight, or major such as getting caught in fire or emergency. In both cases, we land up paying for our ignorance.

Alarms are there to avoid such critical/troublesome situations, to get cautious and alert on time so as to act and respond to them on time. Alarms are all about timing. If they go unacknowledged for a longer duration, they end up in a problematic situation. So it is mandatory to acknowledge and attend to them wisely and on time. Now, the question is –

Do all Alarms have these sound/light effects which get attention easily?

Have you ever heard of "SILENT ALARMS" too?

Let's move from the theoretical image of alarms to the practical image. Alarms are reminders or triggers or notifications that pass on a signal to be cautious, to pay attention, to be alert whenever something disturbing, abnormal, dangerous awaits us. With these parameters in mind, we can conclude that they cannot be limited to being symbolized with sound and lights only. They can also be in the form of circumstances, in the form of experiences, in the form of instances, and in the form of incidences faced by us in our day-to-day life. But to listen to these and to see these, we don't just need our ears and eyes, but the capability of listening to the unsaid and looking at the unseen. We need to observe and we need to react accordingly.

But how to recognize such Silent Alarms?

Why do we judge?

Is it worth being so judgmental?

Is it fine to keep everything under the scanner?

Is it appropriate to analyze each and every situation?

Is it appropriate to judge a person for each and every act?

The answer is of course "NO".

We cannot see everything with doubt and suspicion. But at the same time, we cannot ignore anything that seems to disturb us, that warns us, that demands our attention. Because alarms are for warning and if ignored we may land in big trouble.

Now coming back to our focal point of relations, there is always a possibility when we feel disturbed in a particular relationship. Do these disturbances qualify as Alarms? If it is occasional, it can be overlooked or adjusted. But if it is repetitive, then consistently ignoring it will be similar to ignoring a warning alarm. A consistent feeling of discomfort or disturbance in a particular relationship is a signal of bitterness cropping up. If it is repetitive, or if it is getting magnified then it surely needs to be addressed before it becomes unmanageable.

While encountering any alarms, it is advised to acknowledge them timely as it is best to mitigate the causes of alarms before they land us in a bigger problem. The same goes with these unseen alarms that we sense as a trigger of disturbances. It becomes essential that despite our hesitancy and reluctance of probing further into our relationship for the root cause of conflicts and disturbances, we shall take a step forward and establish open communication and an unbiased mindset to understand the actual reasoning. We can directly discuss with the related person or seek help from another common relation and work on all possible ways to suppress that trigger of disturbance, to re-establish harmony. The concept of acknowledging the alarms here usually help us to resolve misunderstanding in relationships at a very early stage. This timely acknowledgment can clear the fog of doubt easily and help in retaining back the relationship with no grudges. However, as already discussed if you cannot regain your mental peace despite all efforts, do disassociate with that relation. So, I would just like to conclude by saying that:

Never ever ignore any alarming situation,

Never ever ignore toxicity in a relation.

Develop a good vision to visualize,

An unbiased mindset to analyze,

The circumstances, and the disturbances.

Alarms are for responding,

Not for ignoring.

Wake UP!!

And Stay Alert!!

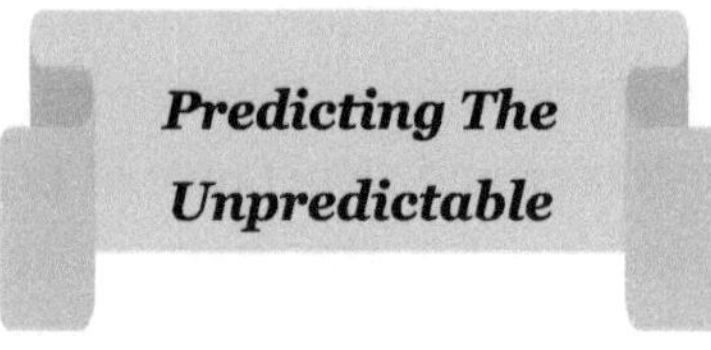

How often have you tried to figure out,

What next...?

What if...?

What's going to happen in the future...?

It is a common question and I think almost everyone is engulfed with such questions at some point in time. Every human tries to predict what's coming ahead, based on situations, based on circumstances, and of course, based on experiences. It is always good to plan your future, to look forward to what lies ahead, to be prepared for what you may have to face tomorrow.

But does life move the way we predict?

The answer is – "NO"

This is because when we look at the future, we frame some 'situation' on our own and predict all pros and cons revolving around that. But the hard reality is that the 'situation' itself is '***Unpredictable.***' So, what we thought may not happen at all.

Now, does that mean we shall only dwell in our present and shall not bother about the future? – "YES/ NO"?

We cannot generalize the question and we cannot generalize the answer. We have to plan certain things. Future planning is necessary to build a steady path and stable life ahead. But we cannot plan and define everything. So, in this quest of future planning, we shall always remember that the world will not move the way we like/we thought it to be. We shall, therefore, leave certain things to move the way they are moving.

Now relating this discussion with our predictability on relationships does emphasize that we usually decide on the future of relation based on present conditions only. But as we grow, as circumstances change, as each one of us gets bound with new responsibilities, new challenges, new targets, and new relations in this walk of life, the impact on our behavior and existing relations is unavoidable. For some of these changes, we all are prepared based on past experiences. For example- The bond of parents and children, where the children spend a lot of time with parents in childhood days but with increasing load of studies, their availability decreases. It is rare that parents will ever complain that our children are so busy in studies that they do not have time to talk to us. But it is equally common that once the children are married, parents will often complain, our children are so busy with their spouse that they have forgotten us. Both scenarios discussed here were predictable. But suppose, the child visits abroad for studies and was so influenced by the life there that he/she plans to seek a job and settle there permanently (even though, it was never ever thought of that he/she will settle in another country), then this comes up as an unexpected unpredictable surprise for parents. In all of these situations, it is possible that the emotional connection stays as is, the respect and love are present, but the time availability is not.

> ***"You can talk with someone for years, everyday, and still, it won't mean as much as what you can have when you sit in front of someone, not saying a word, yet you feel that person with your heart, you feel like you have known the person for forever.... connections are made with the heart, not the tongue."***
>
> ***– C. JoyBell C***

So it will vary for each person that how they will react/respond to such change in relationships. Some may accept it and learn to live with it. Others may keep on complaining about it.

So in relationships, our existing bond with a person may change in terms of physical proximity, emotional connection, ways of expression or behavior, way of communication depending on the changing circumstances around us. As long as the core emotions stay intact and the related people develop good mutual understanding to allow such flexibilities and compromises, things stay well. As said earlier, if we can tune to each other's changing frequencies, we can stay synchronized.

It shall be kept in mind that a mere change does not mean that something in our relationship has changed. Such changes can occur due to any other external or unrelated factor or situation revolving around us. And even though we cannot do much about the future, we shall always refer past and present in unison before framing any opinion.

Let us take a few examples.

The first example is of a happy-go-lucky friend, relative, or colleague with whom you have shared a good bond. However, a tragedy in the family engulfed that person with grief and bereavement and the world no longer appears the same to that person. Dealing with intense emotional turmoil, the behavior of the person for you also changes. This person might not be able to show the same level of care, affection, helping attitude towards you, as the person himself/herself is broken and fragile. They might not be able to participate in your success and celebrations as before, as the intense pain and sadness have made that person numb. Judging such a person for his/her behavior by just focusing on your present relation and behavior will be an injustice. Your past experiences and the type of bond you used to share before that tragedy cannot be ignored. Also, even though you are not directly related to that tragedy but still the present circumstances of that person and the role of those circumstances in manipulating his/her behavior cannot be ignored. This is an unpredictable situation but such are the testing times of core emotions on which a relationship is built. If there is trust, faith, compassion, and empathy, a friend will never hold any grudges for a friend who seems to have changed after facing a tragedy.

Another example can be that of a wedding. As parents, we tend to have the habit of being on priority for our children. We are used to having their undivided attention and also used to have significant control over their lives. However, post-wedding, they establish another relation and it becomes evident that they also need to share time, attention, and decision making with their life partners. This often results in unnecessary conflicts. This sort of relationship adjustment can be easily predicted and a prior mental preparedness for a few compromises is always helpful in keeping up the relationship healthy despite certain changes.

Water flows at its best without obstructions. If we place our finger in the path of flowing water, it swirls here and there. The same goes for life. It is better to let it move the way it is moving, if we try to intervene it starts taking a haphazard, jumbled shape. The same goes with relationships. Trying to take too much control and effort to keep aligning and realigning them usually ends up in disturbances. Sometimes, we lose focus of our actual target and actual track and keep moving round and round in a confined space exploring different possibilities. At times we may also land up converting a smooth clear path into a complex, puzzling road leaving us lost and confused. So, one shall just focus on the harmony of the relationship keeping in view that the core values of the bond shall stay intact and little allowance for deviations based on circumstances shall be allowed. Even though a mother's love for a child never fades, but still a mother cannot keep the child in her lap forever. For professional and personal growth, most of the time the child does need to move away. At such times, it is important to remember, bonds of love and respect are not governed by physical proximity but by emotional connections. Similarly, a close childhood friend who used to share every bit with you may not be able to talk to you for weeks in the future. But that does not mean that the bond of friendship is fading away.

The decision of terming any unpleasant relation as Toxic Relation needs very careful observation as it is a delicate matter of concern. Be very clear and sure before framing any opinions, before making any drastic decisions, before stepping away from a precious relation.

We shall be ready to accept the fact that we don't have control over everything and every day comes with a new beginning, a new challenge, a new change, a new struggle, a new lesson, and a new experience. We shall happily welcome these changes and be ready to accept and face whatever lies ahead.

The above discussions are an effort to throw light on the fact that the way we share and express in relationships may change over a period of time. But a slight change shall not be misunderstood but shall be welcomed and adjusted. This is the essence of true relation.

Chapter Five

Prioritizing Relationships

In previous chapters, we have tried to emphasize the meaning and importance of relationships. Each and every relation is significant with its own meaning, its own necessity, and its own worth. To follow our roles, we have to be faithful in all of them. We have also discussed ways to manage relationships in a better way by following a flexible and understanding approach. But so far, we have been mainly talking about one relation at a time. There are several occasions when conflicts arise due to the mix-up of multiple relationships at once. We need to understand that when we are dealing with a bunch of relations – father, mother, brother, sister, spouse, grandparents, in-laws, uncles, aunts, cousins, nephews, niece, friends, colleagues, neighbors, acquaintances —

How to decide who takes priority over others?

Who is more important?

- Parents/Children/Spouse?
- Friends/Siblings?
- Paternal relatives/Maternal relatives?
- Own relatives/In-laws?

Such confusions, such questions keep coming in our day-to-day life as there are several instances when we are not able to please everybody. However hard we try; it is not possible to please everyone around us all the time.

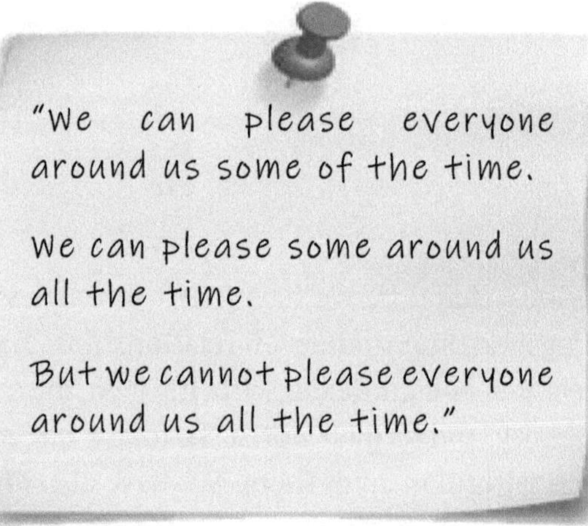

We dwell in dilemma; we think and re-think and we finally proceed to satisfy some when it is not possible to satisfy all. Sometimes we will sail through such tides smoothly while sometimes we will find ourselves drowning in a flood of misunderstandings and complaints from the other side. If the other side stays calm, then also, we may feel the discomfort of not being able to please everyone. If we live with the approach of being a superhuman, an ideal person, a perfect figure, who is committed to doing the best and being the best for everyone around us, we will often find ourselves struggling in such situations. We keep introspecting and questioning ourselves whether we took the right decision or not?

So, isn't it better if we prepare a priority list of our relationships and ease the trouble instead of thinking it over again and again?

So, what are you thinking?

Pick up the pen.

Think of your special ones and start preparing a list based on priority.

You have 15 minutes.

Be honest, prepare the list and thereafter start reading further.

What happened? List prepared?

Case 1: "YES"

Are you satisfied?

"To some extent".

Do you have any doubts/confusions?

"Yes, I am not sure if my priority order is justified or not?"

Do you want to think again?

"No, I don't feel it will solve the problem."

Is the dilemma of choosing amongst relations over?

"No".

Case 2: "NO"

Why?

"There was more and more confusion. There are so many relationships around me. I feel like I am tangled in a spider's web."

Just think over these, one by one, and decide who is more important for you?

"I did think but I am not able to reach any logical conclusion. I don't know if I have to keep my mother on top who bought me into this world, who taught me to crawl and stand and walk? Or, shall I keep my spouse on top, with whom I have committed to share all phases of life, to walk together come what may, to stand by in all joys and sorrows?"

So, you could not move ahead placing one over the other?

"Yes, it's impossible to make a rightful judgment."

This small exercise will help us know for now and forever, that it is practically impossible to prioritize one relation over another. Each one has its own worth and significance attached to it. We cannot just compare one with the other and label one as more important than another.

What is the correct approach then?

Most of our life is spent in maintaining and retaining relationships. But instead of joy and pleasure, they become a burden at times. Sometimes our inability to effectively handle multiple relationships in a justified way creates a lot of mental stress. Conflicts at times become so repetitive or intense that we feel like breaking the chains and running away from all these associations and we start getting afraid of this word "relationship". The word that was meant to be a blessing and act as our support system now becomes a nightmare for us. The most beautiful painting on the canvas of our life, the sweetness and pleasures of beautiful relations, when they become a nightmare for us, our lives become like a barren land.

Instead of being a part of a beautiful garden, where our parents stand like roots, where we stand with our spouse like trees, where our children stand like fruits, where our siblings stand like flowers, where our friends stand like grass, we start feeling like a part of a spider's web in a dark room, tangled badly and searching for an escape route.

So, isn't there any solution to ease out things?

Why not?

If there are problems?

There are solutions as well.

Problems and solutions always co-exist. It is up to us if we can search for that solution or not.

There can be several ways to see the relationships around us.

Approach 1 – Classifying on basis of relation name such as:

- God
- Self
- Parents and Siblings
- Spouse and In-laws
- Relatives
- Friends
- Institutional associations – Teacher, Boss, Colleagues

- Social associations – Neighbours, Service providers (shopkeepers, vendors, helpers)
- Other acquaintances

Approach 2 – Classifying on the basis of relationship needs such as:

- Moral support – Can be parents, spouse, children, few relatives, close friends, etc.
- Financial support – Can be office, parents, spouse, children
- Spiritual support – Can be God, spiritual guides
- Educational support - Can be parents, teachers
- Fun and Entertainment – Can be siblings, friends, colleagues, children

Approach 3 – Classifying on basis of core emotion attached such as:

- Love – Can be parents, spouse, siblings, children
- Care and concern – Can be parents, relatives, spouse, children, siblings
- Respect – Can be parents, elders, parents in law, teachers, spiritual guides, boss
- Trust and Faith – Can be parents, spouse, friends, teachers, spiritual guides
- Compassion and Empathy – Can be parents, spouse, relatives, friends, neighbors
- Satisfaction – Can be employer, customer, service providers, helpers, government

The above approaches and the parameters within are just indicative. You can add to these and you can figure out a totally new approach as well. Now, what do these approaches tell?

The fact is that whenever we have to choose one over the other, we apply one such approach to decide on that. We usually consider ourselves in a single-dimensional plane. We stand at a place and draw lines of distance placing each relation, one after the other. So, we often undergo the dilemma that if one is pulled nearer, the other tends to move farther. We see people around us—family and friends standing at a definite distance in a straight line. It seems as if we have to change the place of one with the other. We often consider creating a vacant space if we want to assign that place to a new person.

But after having a closer look at the multiple experiences and circumstances, we will notice that this outlook shall change. Some of you might already be possessing this new outlook. It is never a conflict of who is near and who is far, who is on the top and who is on the bottom; it is never a conflict of creating/reserving space for each relation and staying stuck to it forever. We meet different people in different phases of life, all of them unique and special in their own way. Also based on our personal circumstances and goals of that particular time, different people may hold a different place in our lives. For instance, our knowledge needs that are initially met by parents, shift to school teachers, coaching mentors, college professors, office seniors, and other guides and influencers depending on our learning areas and requirements, as we keep moving to different phases of our lives. So, we cannot assign one person for a particular need for a lifetime. Also depending on how much this knowledge need holds value for us in the present scenario, decide if the related person will be our close or distant associate. Another example can be that of a “best friend”. If you had a “Best friend” in school, it does not overrule the possibility of getting another “best friend” in college/job, nor does it mean that you are diminishing the value of your already existing “best friend”.

To be able to grasp this concept, one needs to broaden the vision from one-dimensional to three-dimensional. We are the core of a sphere. And we can have multiple relations at the same distance but different angles. We can also have multiple relations at multiple distances resembling several concentric spheres around us. On the circumference of each sphere, there is ample space to accommodate more people. As we will move farther away from the core, this sphere will keep becoming larger. This clearly signifies the presence of limited people who are extremely close to us and a very large number of acquaintances who are farther but numerous. There are several spheres depending on the type of relation and degree of closeness. It is clearly evident now that there will be and can be several people on the same sphere holding the same importance and degree of closeness in our life.

The 3-Dimensional Relationship Sphere

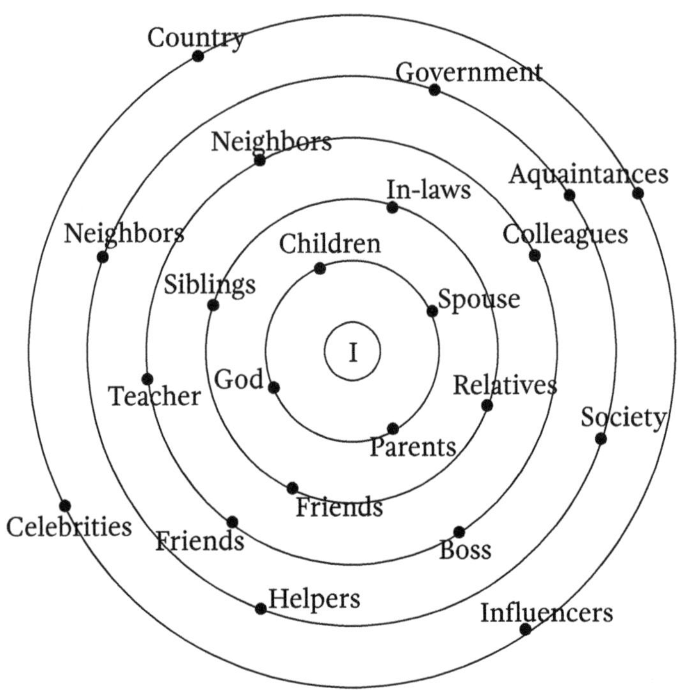

Now, I will put down a few situations, and based on the concepts discussed in this book, I urge the readers to frame their answers-

 # Situation 1

My parents want me to focus only on my academics while my sports teacher recommends that I shall participate in the upcoming Badminton tournament as well?

 # Situation 2

My wife wants to celebrate our anniversary at a Chinese restaurant while my parents recommend visiting a temple and thereafter having traditional dinner at home with close relatives?

 # Situation 3

I am selected as cricket team captain for my office match. My best friend (colleague), wants to be an opening batsman but as captain, I know very well, he won't be fit for the opening.

 # Situation 4

I have committed to spend the weekend with my spouse shopping for the wedding ceremony at my in-law's place. But my mother slipped and has a swollen ankle and needs my help for her daily chores.

 # Situation 5

We are on an international holiday trip. My sibling wants to visit the museum while I want to eat the local food (and we have limited time).

 # Situation 6

My boss told me to work overtime to meet the project deadline but it is coinciding with my nephew's birthday party.

 # Situation 7

I have booked movie tickets with my friend but my father wants me to drive him to the retirement ceremony of his colleague.

 # Situation 8

My spouse wants to invest in shares and mutual funds but my parents suggest investing in property.

 # Situation 9

I promised my family a picnic after a long time but my neighbor asked for urgent help for a medical emergency.

 # Situation 10

Being a doctor family, we all have always expected that my daughter will opt for medical. But she is interested in modeling and acting which my doctor parents highly disagree with.

 # Situation 11

It is pleasant weather and we had planned for a long drive but then my friend calls me and asks for my car to pick up his parents from the airport (as his car broke down).

 # Situation 12

My boss offers me an international on-site assignment of 3 years. My spouse suggests taking it up while my parents suggest denying it.

We will not discuss the answers here, as there is not always a single best solution for situational questions. The motto is that the solution opted by you shall satisfy you. However, if the essence behind the concept of this book is absorbed by you, I am sure that you are now in a position to narrow down the complexity of prioritizing relationships. I don't know if this will satisfy all of you or not but in my view, there is a simple solution.

Prioritization depends on perception, perspective, and circumstances. It cannot follow a thumb rule. It needs subjective evaluation, unbiased decision-making, and wise judgment.

Always remember

We never have to choose between "RELATIONSHIPS"

...

We have to choose between "CIRCUMSTANCES".

We never have to choose between "WHO" needs us most...

We have to choose between "WHAT" needs us most.

Relationship bonds are not meant to be treated as battleground or court...

Relationship bonds shall be treated like a temple where everyone shall be respected and pleased.

WHERE EVERYONE WINS...

BUT NO ONE LOSES!!

We never have to choose who is "RIGHT" or who is "WRONG" ...

We have to decide on the unbiased, logical, and rational approach...

We never have to win arguments... we have to win hearts!!

Epilogue

We started with the basic definition of relationships and then dived deep into the sea of relationships to gather insights on why relationships are important for each one of us, what are several categories or types of relations we see around us, how to manage them effectively to maintain harmony and how to simultaneously deal with multiple relations effectively? We are now here with an in-depth understanding of the core and detailed definition of relationships. We are now in a capacity to categorize them on the basis of explicit or implicit (by birth or selective), wanted or unwanted, harmonious or toxic, and on the basis of relationship name, need, emotion, etc. We have explored several methodologies to effectively maintain and manage healthy and balanced relationships. We have shared several day-to-day life examples and situations to move from the theoretical to the practical approach.

So, what is the key takeaway, the final formula?

Formula, Equations, Theorems, Derivations, Rules, Protocols – We have them all around us guiding us.

Can we really develop a formula to maintain healthy relationships?

Can we conclude with a set of instructions, a collection of guidelines?

Well, we cannot limit such abstract topics to the boundaries of the mathematical formulas, or pre-defined rules and protocols. Yes, there can be some protocols established by society. These are passed on from generation to generation based on the experiences of our ancestors. Also, we are well aware that applying any formula or set of rules is not so easy. All of them do come with certain conditions, limitations, and exceptions. If we ignore them, we will land up with wrong results.

In our efforts to maintain healthy relationships, we will often encounter questions regarding,

What to do?
How to do it?
Where to do?
When to do it?
Why do?

But we cannot have a definite answer for such questions. We need to understand that life, emotions, and relationships do not come with a set protocol. The already established framework also needs recalculation based on present circumstances. Applying a rigid thumb rule to your life, emotions or relationships end up making things more complex and unmanageable. Just like any other formula or theorem, such protocols will also have certain conditions, limitations, and exceptions. If we overlook them, we will end up with wrong decisions.

With this what I am trying to emphasize is that when the rules and protocols and expectations are inherited from society and not looked upon independently with an unbiased mindset, then conflicting situations may arise often. As can be seen from situation examples discussed earlier, relationship priorities may toggle from time to time depending on circumstances.

Our focus shall not be on superficial actions but on the core emotions that build our relationships. Now, these emotions are the foundation stones of our bonding or relationship with another person.

When we cannot measure emotions, how can we measure the weightage of relationships?

How can we prioritize one over the other?

How can we place one on top and the other on the bottom?

How can we say one is important and the other is not?

Can we measure Love?

Can we measure Affection?

Can we measure Care?

Can we measure Respect?

Can we measure Relationships?

NO

These are precious treasures.
These are priceless.
Do not diminish their value,
By trying to weigh them,
By trying to measure them,
By trying to prioritize one over the other.

Redefine Relationships

Where each relation is
A reflection of Love and Affection
A reflection of Trust and Faith
A reflection of Care and Concern
A reflection of Respect and Honour,
Do not obstruct these reflections
Allow every ray to glow
To reach you freely
To radiate around you vibrantly
Let this Aura fill your world
With limitless brightness

As the foundation blocks of relationships are emotions, a good understanding of effectively dealing with emotions also comes up as a helping tool in maintaining healthy relationships. The way nutritious food builds better immunity to fight diseases and keep us healthy, in a similar manner positive thoughts, good understanding, and effective management of emotions builds a strong foundation to deal with day-to-day conflicts of relationships and ultimately resolve them to regain harmony.

I would recommend readers to read my other book on "Decoding Emotions" for mastering the art of appraising and exhibiting emotions in daily life. Also, if you or someone related to you is dealing with intense emotions of Grief, you can find some comfort by reading my book on "Grief", an unpleasant journey. The most crucial and critical stage of our lives is when we feel hopeless and helpless and I hope none of us shall reach that stage. But if you or anyone related to you is actually dealing with such extremes of hopelessness, self-destruction, or suicidal thoughts, do not hesitate to seek help and free yourself from such thoughts. There is often a hesitancy in seeking external help on such matters. I have done my effort of compiling a book, 'Self Love', that will help you combat the feeling of self-destruction and suicide.

We have talked enough about relationships and emotions. It is time to sit back, relax and ponder over to derive the best in our relationships. So, I will conclude here with the hope that I have been successful in building a good author-reader relationship with you.

> ***"The relationship between reader and writer is reciprocal in a way. We co-create each other. We are constantly emerging out of the relationship we have with others."***
>
> ***– Ruth Ozeki***

Let's take an oath to do our best to maintain harmony around us, which seems to start at an individual level but step by step, it will grow as a chain reaction reflecting positive vibes all around, thus making this entire world a better place to live in.

"When you cultivate quality relationships, not only do you feel better and help your friends feel better, but you contribute to an increase of joy, love, and peace in the world."

– Tara Bianca

HOPE YOU LIKED THE BOOK

Did this book help you in a better understanding of relationships?

Send your feedback, suggestions, and insights. We would love to hear your experiences about complex relationship conflicts that you have come across.

Do write to us if you want to touch upon any unexplored or unanswered questions on relationships experienced by us.

To reach the author:

https://akanksharastogi.wordpress.com/

feedback4aa@gmail.com

Other Titles from Author

Non-Fiction, Self-help books

SELF LOVE: Combat feelings of self-destruction and suicide

This is a self-help book, mainly to deal with depressive and suicidal thoughts. Frequently experiencing feelings of low self-esteem, anxiety, depression, or suicidal thoughts is an alarm to remind - take extra care of yourself. Do not abandon yourself, it is time to love yourself, accept your feelings, talk about them, and find ways to deal with them. The book explores multiple dimensions associated with such feelings and discusses practical ways to manage and cope with them. The book is penned to approach this aspect with a focus on self-initiative and explicitly discuss hesitation and unwillingness at each step. An effort to overcome these roadblocks to move on a path of self-love initiates self-healing and helps to gradually mitigate the toxicity of negative thoughts. This book conveys a strong message of respecting one's life and induce self-love to overcome suicidal thoughts and depression. ***This book is available in two versions – Paperback and Kindle.***

GRIEF: An Unpleasant Journey

This is a self-help book that discusses the emotional turmoil of a grieving person. How does the unexpected shock start a new but rough journey of depression, helplessness, and hopelessness? How one feels captivated in a never-ending storm of such discomforting feelings? What type of external supports or comments actually soothe in such instances and what ends up hurting even more? Why do most of the people struggling with such emotions prefer to be socially isolated? Why and how do the gradual feelings of acceptance get wiped away putting back the grieving person from where they started? Is there a way to stop the cycling of these emotions back and forth? Why do some people seem to cope up easily while some find it very difficult? Can everlasting acceptance be achieved? Or will the grief leave its imprints for a lifetime?

There are endless questions without a definitive answer. This book is an effort to address some of these based on the author's personal experience. The book will be of immense help to friends and family of a grieving person to let them understand the thoughts of a grieving mind and how to soothe it.

DECODING EMOTIONS: Master the art of appraising and exhibiting emotions in daily life

This is a self-help book that aims to empower the readers to get accustomed to different emotions. Have you ever wondered or noticed the millions of emotions in and around us? Some soothe us like the calm wind; some refresh us like the sprinkling rain. Some burn us like the scorching sun; some uproot us like the massive storm. It is worth pondering over the countless, immeasurable, invisible entities (emotions) inside us and around us (emotions of our community), which often create a roadmap for our behavior, expressions, decisions, and actions? Being able to differentiate amongst several emotions that appear to resemble each other supports in unnecessary entwining of emotions. This book uniquely categorizes emotions and explains the concept with simple, day-to-day life examples, making it light, interesting, thought-provoking, and a knowledgeable read. ***This book is available in two versions – Paperback and Kindle.***

Children's Fiction books

Titles in Amazing Apes series

Amazing Apes Series consists of humorous children's fiction books with interesting pictures. All books of this series are available in two versions – Colored and Economy (Black & White) Edition. These books are suitable for age-group 6 to 12 years, Grade 2nd to 6th.

The story is about the amazing apes residing in Paradisiaca Island. Five little amazing apes - Chimpanio, Spiclu, Banny, Princess Velutina, and Gibbon together solve various mysteries.

THE MYSTERY OF ROSE PERFUME

The exciting school picnic day takes a terrible turn when some students break the rules. The fun and frolic at the amusement park turn into trouble for the students and their teacher Mrs. Furry. How will the five amazing apes, solve the mystery behind the sweet fragrance of Red Rose Perfume?

BIG SURPRISE

This Children's Day became super exciting when King Musa announced a Big Surprise for children. But at the last moment, the surprise appears to turn into a Flop Show. Will Spiclu, Velutina, Banny, Gibbon, and Chimpanio be able to set it right?

THE MYSTERY OF GHOST TREE

The story behind the 200 years old Ghost Tree in Paradisiaca Public School is known to all. But do ghosts really exist? Has anyone seen them? What happens when Chimpanio, Banny, Gibbon, Spiclu, Velutina decide to unravel The Mystery Of Ghost tree?

INVISIBLE GLUE

When Spiclu's invention that is used to play a prank on the teacher, later helps to save Paradisiaca Island from evil plans of the enemy, all applaud the amazing five superstars - Chimpanio, Banny, Gibbon, Spiclu, Velutina. What is this secret invention? How does it help to save the island from enemies?

Titles in Tara short stories series

TARA'S MAGIC PILLOW

Tara's Magic Pillow is a collection of four interesting short stories with a moral message.

- Tara's Magic Pillow
- Tara's Birthday Party
- Tara's Lucky Charm
- Tara's Torch Genie

There are interesting things that happen in these stories and each incident teaches a small lesson to little Tara. The stories are full of fun and surprise.

- Tara Meets Mermaid
- Tara And Fluffy
- Tara And Jugnoo
- Tara's Mitthu

These books are good for children of age group 3 to 9 years. The stories can also be read out by parents to their little children.

COMING SOON!!!

The mystery and adventure series

"The INCREDIBLE 8"

Meet the Incredible-8 gang -

Jolly, Tubby, Brill, Charmy, Witto, David, Eliza and Parry, the Parrot,

who land up into unexpected adventures and end up solving mysteries in an incredible way...

www.ingramcontent.com/pod-product-compliance
Ingram Content Group UK Ltd.
Pitfield, Milton Keynes, MK11 3LW, UK
UKHW041957190726
13854UKWH00005B/2021

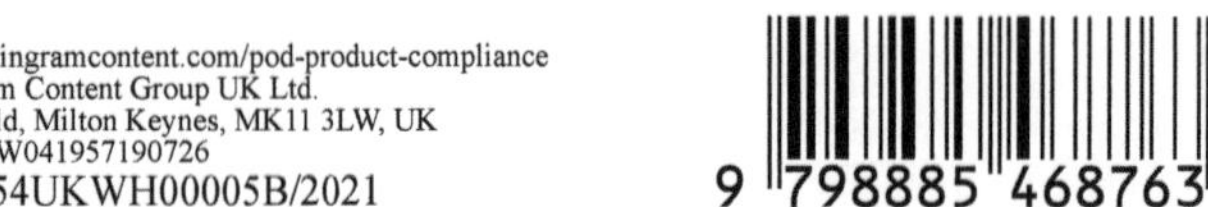

9 798885 468763